The Art and Craft of Teaching

Edited by Margaret Morganroth Gullette

Distributed for the
Harvard-Danforth Center for Teaching and Learning,
Faculty of Arts and Sciences, Harvard University
by
Harvard University Press
Cambridge, Massachusetts
1984

Library of Congress Cataloging in Publication Data
Main entry under title:

The Art and craft of teaching.

Includes index.
1. College teaching—Addresses, essays, lectures.
I. Gullette, Margaret Morganroth.
LB2331.A646 1984   378'.125   84-625
ISBN 0-674-04680-3

*Teaching is like dropping ideas into
the letter box of the human subconscious.
You know when they are posted but you
never know when they will be received
or in what form.*

This book is dedicated to C. Roland (Chris) Christensen
by his grateful students,
who want him to know that the letters he posts do arrive.

This collection of essays was originally published by the Harvard-Danforth Center for Teaching and Learning, an office of the Faculty of Arts and Sciences at Harvard. That publication was made possible by a grant from a fund donated by Dr. Ansel Kinney ('20, A.M. '21, Ph.D. '23), a long-time friend of Harvard University. His fund has made life easier for young people at crucial moments in their graduate training, and we hope that the dissemination of this collection will further that aim as well.

The editor and authors of *The Art and Craft of Teaching* wish to thank President Derek Bok for his assistance. His enthusiasm, his creativity, and his gift of a grant made the original edition possible. The editor expresses her appreciation also to those of her teachers who, like Chris Christensen, made teaching seem the most absorbing, crucial, and disinterested of callings: Betty Morganroth, Florence Sayer, Stephen Orgel, Richard Poirier, Stephen Booth, Paul Alpers, Warner Berthoff, and Robert Lowell.

Contents

Preface

Few might expect a book about teaching to emerge from the Faculty of Arts and Sciences at Harvard University. While generations of students have been taught by gifted and talented teachers, those teachers have seldom written about the process of teaching. It was considered an art to be practiced rather than a set of skills to be discussed. But this has been changing.

In 1975, with the support of President Derek Bok and a three-year grant from the Danforth Foundation, the Harvard Center for Teaching and Learning was established. There were some grumblings. One senior member of the faculty recommended returning the grant, because accepting it implied that teaching at Harvard was less than ideal. In spite of an occasional protest, an overwhelming majority of the faculty readily agreed that college teaching is one of the few professions for which no training is provided, and that this should be changed. With the goal of helping faculty, especially young faculty, to develop the necessary skills, the Center developed a range of programs. One question was whether Harvard instructors would get involved in them. That question has now been answered by thousands of teachers, who have. And in 1980, by vote of the faculty, the Center was given a permanent status.

In the eight years of its existence the Center's programs have involved instructors in various ways. Over a hundred gifted Harvard professors, for example, have participated in our Professional Training Series (a series of panel discussions about many aspects of teaching). The stellar roster has included John Kenneth Galbraith on "How I Could Have Done Much Better," David Riesman on "The Role of Teaching in the Scholarly Life," and B. F. Skinner on "Writing and the Teaching of Writing." The list is extensive and impressive; it also includes William Alfred, Bernard Bailyn, Daniel Bell, Andrew Gleason, Stephen Jay Gould, Stanley Hoffmann, Wallace MacCaffrey, Edwin Reischauer, Barbara Rosenkrantz, Henry Rosovsky, Judith Shklar, Frank Westheimer, and James Q. Wilson. These presentations have been preserved on videotapes so that they will continue to be available to generations of teachers.

Another major element of the Center has been the work of the Video Laboratory, where teachers of all ranks can have their classes videotaped. Reviewing one's tape with a counselor leads to significant and observable changes in teaching behaviors and styles. When we contrast the initial taping with subsequent ones, everyone—beginning with the instructor—can easily see the improvements that have taken place. Instructors find this highly encouraging, and it also raises their ratings on student evaluations.

Our work is now sufficiently mature that we have begun a research program to understand the teaching function better. Using our collection of videotapes, we are examining gender differences and helping teachers to avoid gender stereotypes. We are also exploring muddles—situations when everyone talks at once—and finding out who causes them, and showing how to take control.

Of all the workshops, orientations, and seminars that the Center has sponsored, no program has been more memorable than the faculty seminar offered by C. Roland Christensen. President Bok, who had suggested to Professor Christensen that his seminar on teaching at the Business School would be a useful experience for instructors in the Faculty of Arts and Sciences, also had the idea of producing a collection of essays on teaching to be written by participants in the Christensen seminar. *The Art and Craft of Teaching* was created with the aim of making their common know-how available to a larger audience. We hope you find it valuable.

Dean K. Whitla
Director, Harvard-Danforth Center
for Teaching and Learning

Introduction

C. Roland Christensen

This is a book about the practicalities of teaching. We are exposed to teaching throughout our lives; many of our readers (perhaps all of you) have chosen it as your vocation. Despite this exposure and this intention, many teachers know little about teaching, or feel that they know little about it, or both. We hope that you will finish reading this book with new confidence and new resources.

In the first essay, James Wilkinson states our aim as teachers, describes our most common problem of preparation, and finely states the authors' objectives in producing the present book:

> In order to avoid the pitfalls of poor teaching, teachers themselves must learn to communicate what they know and respond to the needs of their students. Teaching skills, like private student projects, are often assembled at random. The following chapters are an attempt to do for the teacher what formal instruction does for the student: provide a struc-

C. ROLAND CHRISTENSEN is George F. Baker, Jr., Professor of Business Administration, Harvard University. He has been a visiting member of the faculties of IMEDE (Institut pour l'Etude des Méthodes de Direction de l'Entreprise, Lausanne), the Stanford University Business School, the Sloan School at M.I.T. and the Harvard Law School. He is a Fellow in the Academy of Management, and a member of the Society for Public Administration, the Academy of Political Science and the Organizational Behavior Teaching Society. He is also a chairman of the faculty board of advisors to IMEDE and director of several business organizations. He is the author of *Management Succession in Small and Growing Enterprises* (1953) and *Teaching By the Case Method* (1982), and is co-author of *Business Policy, Text and Cases* (5th edition, 1982); *Problems in General Management* (1961); *Policy Formulation and Administration* (8th edition, 1980); and *The Motivation, Productivity and Satisfaction of Workers* (1958). A member of the faculty of the Harvard Business School since 1946, his research interests center on improving the effectiveness of boards of directors; his teaching interests focus on field studies in business policy and discussion leading.

ture, initiate a dialogue, and propose new standards of excellence and a "sense of style."

When President Eliot gave his inaugural address in 1869,
he reviewed the Harvard scene and concluded that "the problem
to be solved is not what to teach but how to teach." The problem of 1869 is still with us 100 years later; we make progress
slowly. In an effort to solve the problem with more appropriate
speed, President Bok and the Harvard-Danforth Center for
Teaching and Learning, under the direction of Dean Whitla
and Margaret Gullette, have been engaged for the past eight
years in a program to improve instruction. That program is
already having an impact on Harvard's teaching standards.

As one part of this program, the Harvard-Danforth Center
and the Harvard Graduate School of Business Administration
have since 1976 sponsored a seminar on discussion-leading,
which I teach. It has been an enjoyable collaborative effort,
which brings together discussion teachers from the Faculty of
Arts and Sciences and many professional schools.

This seminar, "Developing Discussion Leadership Skills,"
has been based on a number of critical assumptions. First, and
most important, we took as given that the instructor had an
in-depth command of the knowledge and/or skills he or she
wished to teach, as well as a command of basic course concepts
and organization. Second, we assumed that the course dealt
with material where discussion—teacher-to-student and student-
to-student dialogue—was a critically important part of the
teaching and learning process. Finally, we assumed that the
instructor was sincerely interested in helping students learn.

Given those three circumstances, our hypothesis was that
effective section teaching was dependent on the artistry of the
instructor, that that artistry/skill consisted of mastering details,
and that those skills could be observed, abstracted and taught to
other instructors. The longer I have taught, the more I have
been fascinated by those aspects of discussion leadership which
manifest themselves in class after class: which student's hand
should the instructor recognize, what type of question should
be asked at what time, what kind of response should the instructor make to various specific student comments, what does
one write on the greenboard, when does one summarize, and
how does one "pace" the class in discussion? Personal observation of countless discussion sessions, enriched by the contributions of several hundred participants in Business School semi-

nars, produced a "bank" of skills, techniques and attitudes which we thought would be of use to instructors in a wide variety of academic fields. One could, we concluded, teach discussion teaching.

The eight authors of these essays were all colleagues in this Harvard-Danforth Center/Harvard Business School teaching seminar. Each author brings understanding and experience to the topic about which she or he is writing. All are professionals devoted to the improvement of their fields—disciplines which range from economics and history to sociology and ethics.

Their advice is not abstract, but directly related to what they have experienced in the classroom. While writing the book, they also met over a period of months in a remarkable collaboration—a series of argumentative, thorough and frank discussions about teaching in which they compared experiences, discussed formulations, and worked toward a consensus on the central points at issue. Later, everyone had the opportunity to comment on everyone else's essay. Each essay retains its own lively individuality, and the divergences of point of view can be illuminating. In general, the collection offers the cumulative wisdom of the group on a range of essential topics.

Many of my seminar participants have observed that the typical book about teaching has been of limited value to them in the early stages of their teaching careers. The problem may be that the teacher-authors tend, very understandably, to write about the latest challenge they have faced and conquered. The curious beginner, however, would typically like to learn first what the teacher-authors learned first: the chance of using the advice in an actual class is much higher. It is for this reason that all of the articles in this book are written to, and about, the problems and opportunities faced by new instructors. You will find that the essays deal with many of the basic issues you will be facing in the next weeks and years. But do not close the volume even if you already have many years of experience in the classroom; there is always something to learn from dedicated teachers who have taken the time to analyze and explain their procedures. And read on even if you prefer to lecture; several chapters are addressed directly to lecturers, and the others may help you to expand your repertory of teaching styles.

The first chapter introduces us to a typology of different teaching methods. Jim Wilkinson in his "Varieties of Teaching" postulates that different kinds of learning require different methods of teaching and reviews with us the strengths and weaknesses of each method. Jeff Wolcowitz next gives us many suggestions for planning the first class meeting. In detail, he demonstrates how critical it is to establish a workable teacher-student contract, both by explicit "game rules" and by your own classroom behavior. Heather Dubrow and Jim Wilkinson then consider "The Theory and Practice of Lectures." Their concluding recommendation, to have one or two of your lectures videotaped, is an extremely practical suggestion.

The next two chapters are devoted primarily to various aspects of a course that is run mainly through discussion. Appropriately, Tom Kasulis' lead-off chapter concerns "Questioning." Questions and the responses to questions provide the core of any discussion; they are the discussion leader's primary educational tools. What Tom Kasulis does is to illustrate the infinite complexity of asking a simple question and of responding effectively to students when they answer.

The delicate role of the section leader as a link between professor and student is explored in Ullica Segerstråle's chapter. She outlines the multiple functions and challenges of the section instructor and concludes:

> The secret of section leading is not the thorough mastery of the material by the section leader and the transfer of her or his interpretations to the students, but the creation of a context of *organized spontaneity*. The good section leader gives the students opportunities and incentives to express themselves and develop skills within the otherwise somewhat passive context of a lecture course.

Chapter Six, "The Rhythms of the Semester," should be not only read but savored. Laura Nash's hypothesis is that "the richness of a course will depend largely on the professor's willingness to perceive the semester as a teaching unit, and develop the course to exploit its unity." Using the imagery of the dance, she invites us to explore her thesis:

> The component parts of the semester can be likened to the parts of the dance performance, with the melody equal to the subject matter, the staging to the classroom, the mode to the distinctive academic style of the professor, and the dancers to those who participate in the class: students and teacher. Timing, pace, theme, and variation—the formal components of a musical score and its performance—might well be applied to the semester. . . . Thus the teacher is transformed from presenter of wisdom to dancer and composer, responsible for the music and for the way in which the dancers all work their art.

Heather Dubrow, in Chapter Seven, shifts our attention from classroom leadership of a discussion to the instructor's role in helping individual students improve their writing skills— clearly a critical responsibility of any academic institution. Her suggestions for working with students on writing skills are detailed and practical; we all can use her wisdom.

In Chapter Eight Chris Jedrey deals with an important challenge for all instructors—the necessity of evaluating performance and assigning grades. Grading is not a task enjoyed by most academics. It is especially difficult in a discussion setting. As Chris Jedrey points out:

> What are we grading—frequency of comments, enthusiasm, ability to forward the discussion or the individual tour de force—and how? . . . In any case, in a section with twenty or thirty or more students any attempt to evaluate individual contributions to the discussion fairly will require some sort of record-keeping system.

And, in this complicated business of evaluation/grading, we might do well to remember what Walter Jackson Bate wrote in his biography of Samuel Johnson:

> There is a tendency in human nature, whenever we are considering the lives of others, to expect them to proceed at a far brisker pace than we ourselves do, not because we are uncharitable but because our vicarious interest is better able to notice results than to share the actual process and daily crawl of other people's experience.

Bate's plea is not for "softness" or minimal standards; rather, he reminds us to understand the difficulty—even pain—which many experience in the learning process.

Finally, Dick Fraher deals with the central problem: how do we as teachers learn? He gives special attention to the support resources available to a beginning teacher. His secondary theme concerns the evolving role of the instructor as she or he moves through the early years of a teaching career. In considering these subjects he provides support for the ideas advanced earlier in the book by Ullica Segerstråle and Laura Nash.

Dick Fraher appropriately concludes this book on the theme of the learning teachers must attempt. The ultimate test of your classroom abilities may well be not how much you have taught, but how much you have learned and the degree to which your students have learned to learn.

Henry Merritt Wriston, the eighth President of Lawrence University, put the point well in his inaugural address:

A student does not come to college primarily to learn things, to store an intellectual garret with an assortment of odds and ends. He comes to college to learn how to learn, what to learn, where to learn and why to learn.

Arnold Schoenberg makes the point within a wider teacher-student context in the Foreword to the *Harmonielehre* (1922):

What is in this book was learned from my pupils. When teaching it was never my aim merely to tell the pupil what I know. Rather, what *he* did not know. But even that—enough in itself to make me invent something new for each pupil—was not the main thing; I strove to show him the essence of the matter starting from the simplest things. So, as far as I was concerned, there were never these rigid rules which so conscientiously entwine themselves around the pupil's brain. Everything was broken down into instructions, which bind the pupil no more than the teacher. If the pupil can do it better without the instructions, then let him do without them. But the teacher must have the courage to be wrong. His task is not to prove infallible, knowing everything and never going wrong, but rather inexhaustible, ever seeking and perhaps, sometimes finding. Why want to be a demigod? Why not, rather, be a complete man?

To close on a more personal note: welcome to a joyous profession. Teaching, for this instructor, is the greatest of all vocations, for it keeps one well anchored to the world of youth, growth, ideas, search and learning. And teaching is especially exciting in those courses where the discussion mode is the primary educational tool. Providing guidance for the discussion of an article, a book, a poem or an economic problem is a stimulating intellectual assignment. The opportunity to open minds, to develop lines of reasoning, to debate points of view provides one with the opportunity to be an everyday alchemist.

Many students of teaching would say, quite accurately, that after all is said, we don't know the final formula for effective teaching—we can't explain why some instructors have success while others have so many difficulties. And if we know little about teaching we know even less about learning. My favorite description of this complicated interactive process is a paraphrase of a statement by Amy Lowell:

Teaching is like dropping ideas into the letter box of the human subconscious. You know when they are posted but you never know when they will be received or in what form.

The hope of all connected with this book is that these essays will give you some preliminary guidance on the challenges of teaching, and respect for the beauty and generosity involved in leading an effective discussion.

CHAPTER ONE

Varieties of Teaching

James Wilkinson

It is a mistake to assume that all college learning occurs in the classroom. College students learn in many ways; most are able to learn readily and happily even when left to themselves. With nothing but personal interest to spur them on, they may explore the novels of Jane Austen, collect fossils, or immerse themselves in local politics. Informal contacts in the college community, ranging from casual conversations over coffee to deep and lasting friendships, introduce them to ideas and values that may prove as important for their education as their formal course of study. Such unstructured learning is actively promoted by the many American colleges and universities that require undergraduates to live in residence for part or all of four years and that provide space and funds for extracurricular activities. Education, they acknowledge, is not confined to the classroom alone.

What, then, does the teacher contribute to the process of learning that students cannot supply on their own? At least three important things. As the intermediary between the class and a body of knowledge, he or she offers each student structure, evaluation, and support. Structure comes through the teacher's ability to anticipate the likely trouble spots ahead, and willingness to help students find and maintain a realistic pace until they have mastered (or at least reviewed) a coherent body of work. The insights that come from unsupervised reading and extracurricular activities, however intense, are often random experiences; they cannot duplicate the careful sequence and sustained growth of ideas fostered by a well-crafted course. The

JAMES WILKINSON is a Research Associate at the Center for European Studies at Harvard and the holder of a Guggenheim Fellowship. His teaching and research interests lie in the area of modern European intellectual history. For seven years he served as Head Tutor in History and Literature at Harvard and taught in the History Department. He is the author of *The Intellectual Resistance in Europe,* published by Harvard University Press in 1981.

teacher also provides the critique and stimulation of dialogue. Students will be required not only to absorb the instructor's explanations but also to answer questions, to defend a position or react to criticism. Such probing often reveals fundamental gaps in knowledge or misconceptions that must be pointed out before they can be corrected. Finally, a teacher's interest and encouragement can play a crucial role in motivating students to reach beyond self-imposed limits. By participating in the give and take of a learning community, under the guidance of an experienced leader, students share in group resources that usefully supplement their own, and must confront standards that can be ignored or evaded when studying alone.

The concept of "structured dialogue," then, defines education on its most basic level. Through it the teacher seeks to train students in certain skills—writing, textual analysis, quantitative reasoning—that cannot be learned in the abstract, divorced from specific subject matter. The causes of the French Revolution, Hamlet's attitude toward his father, the properties of quadratic equations or the function of hemoglobin hold center stage during the course. Yet except for the small number of students destined to become historians, Shakespeare scholars, mathematicians, or biochemists, the lasting value of what is taught is likely to be a general set of mind that remains even when the particulars of the subject matter have become blurred. William James noted the importance of what he termed "transfer of training"—taking skills learned in one context and applying them to another. Such general skills and attitudes are what the student will retain long after most dates, facts, and equations have been forgotten or superseded.

The number of desirable goals to which teachers may devote their efforts is very large, and teachers by no means agree about their relative merits. Yet at the heart of college teaching, many would argue, lies the attempt to transform how students observe and interpret the world. The teacher's aim is to help them assume an active and creative relationship with their daily environment by developing skills in the three areas of perception, analysis, and expression. By the end of their college years students should be able to identify and define the specifics of a problem or topic, make judgments about their value and importance, and convey those judgments with sufficient clarity that others readily grasp what they mean. The skills and qualities of mind required for these complex operations they will continue to develop and refine for the rest of their lives.

Basic to any intellectual achievement is curiosity—variously described as the "desire to know," or the "urge for discovery." Many students already possess this capacity when they arrive at college, and need only to have it confirmed and nurtured. But this is not always easy. All too often, as freshmen adjust to the formal requirements of academic life and lose their awe of its institutions, they lose sight of the curiosity that brought them there as well. In addition, teachers must in some cases try to awaken a dormant curiosity that has remained asleep even during secondary school; poor teaching at a lower level requires truly superior teaching in college for its effects to be overcome. We also want students to develop a tolerance for the complex and the ambiguous that few have attained before they enter college. To acknowledge the validity of competing and often contradictory points of view, to accept the limited nature of what can be known with certainty, to resist the temptation to reduce the world to simplistic categories of good and bad, white and black—all this requires a sophistication that must be acquired gradually. The teacher's difficult task is thus to keep the student's initial drive and enthusiasm intact while thwarting her or his desire to be content with easy answers.

The teacher also needs to awaken and encourage a critical outlook—skepticism toward unproven assertions, a fine eye for tautologies and self-contradiction—that will serve as a testing mechanism for all that the student encounters. "How do we know?" should become a question that the student asks without prompting. During adult life, Descartes' methodical doubt will prove to be a fundamental asset. At the same time, such criticism implies an alternative standard. It is up to the teacher to demonstrate what that standard is. This can be done primarily by introducing the student to examples of excellence —whether embodied in a sonnet, a code of laws, or a mathematical proof—and by examining their virtues in sufficient detail that they become familiar to the class. Even if students themselves cannot achieve work on this level, its existence serves as a touchstone for judging the efforts of others later on.

The art of expression is cultivated more explicitly in the college setting than are skills of perception or judgment. From freshman English composition to senior honors theses, students are called upon to articulate their thoughts and are graded on the result. But while paper comments can provide them with important lessons on the fine points of spelling, word choice, and use of sources, the larger questions of structure and analysis are often harder for them to grasp, and require correspondingly greater emphasis. How to argue a point and not simply present data; how to link arguments in a logical chain; how to sum up with a sure sense of what is essential and what is merely extrinsic to your case are skills that require coaching and practice. In addition, students need to be helped to present their ideas with grace and to strive for the control, confidence, and economy of means that help make up what Alfred North Whitehead once termed a "sense of style." Here models play as crucial a role as they do in the concept of excellence.

Just as different kinds of learning take place in a college community, so there exists a variety of teaching formats as well —each best suited to conveying a particular combination of skills and attitudes. The three principal vehicles for college instruction are the lecture, the laboratory session or field trip, and the discussion class. Although they share the same general aims embodied in the "structured dialogue," the teaching approach that each type of instruction requires is in some ways unique. A good lecturer may experience problems leading a successful discussion; the discussion leader skilled in asking questions may feel ill at ease when conducting a monologue from the lecture podium. But it should be a teacher's goal to master the full scale of teaching styles, and to know the strengths and drawbacks of each. The balance of this chapter will consider teaching in a comparative context. What are the special characteristics of the tools at the teacher's command?

The immediate advantage of lecturing lies in the clarity of exposition and the breadth of coverage that it allows. Especially as an introduction to a field, lectures can convey a great deal of material efficiently and memorably to a large number of listeners. Thus they are also well suited to demonstrate the art of expression. A lecture that is logically ordered and carefully paced offers students a model of how to subdivide a topic into smaller units and arrange them intelligibly. The aesthetic element inherent in a good lecture—clarity, wit, variety, the revealing detail and the dramatic conclusion—constitutes practical training in a "sense of style." At the same time, the lecturer who conveys a spirit of excitement and who stimulates the student to go further in pursuit of some more specialized area of concern aids in developing curiosity and appreciation for complexity. Every lecture provides a chance to show students the pleasure and exhilaration that come from an imaginative encounter with ideas.

To a greater degree than the leader of a discussion course, the teacher in a lecture hall enjoys direct control over what happens there. She or he decides what topics to present, in what sequence, and in what detail. He or she must also provide the energy that brings the class to life and keeps it lively. A bad lecturer will make poor use of this opportunity for control and allow the class to lose its concentration, succumbing to boredom and perplexity. But even a good lecturer cannot create an extensive dialogue between teacher and student. The same control and responsibility that characterize the lecturer's role inevitably mean that the student's participation will be largely passive. While students may ask questions after class or during office hours, they can reply to lectures only on examinations or in papers. The strength of the lecture is in presenting an example and in generating a stimulus, not in shaping the response. It solicits further work, but does not in itself demand it. For all its focused energy and dramatic power,[1] the lecture alone cannot meet all pedagogical needs.

Because of this, many lecture courses are accompanied by laboratory sessions, field trips, or discussion meetings. All these extend and complement the lecturer's formal presentation. Labs and field trips offer the great advantage of direct contract with the materials discussed in lecture. But in addition to their illustrative value, they can play a major role in training perception. The phenomena that the students confront outside the lecture hall, whether plant specimens, examples of town planning, or a Cézanne still life, possess a complexity and richness that force the students to discriminate between first impressions and underlying patterns, between form and detail. Equally important, students can recognize the distance that separates raw data from the schematic clarity of a lecture diagram. Discovering how few experimental readings lie directly on the predicted curve is a first step toward learning how to relate conceptual categories to an untidy reality. The notebooks, sketches, and laboratory reports that students may be required to submit as the semester progresses allow the instructor to follow their growth in this direction and, where necessary, to offer needed correctives. And as a monitor of student responses, the section leader can alert the lecturer if he or she perceives a major area of difficulty that should be taken up before the class as a whole.

1. For a more detailed discussion of lecturing, see Chapter Three, "The Theory and Practice of Lectures," by Heather Dubrow and James Wilkinson, pp. 25–37.

Discussion sections based on a lecturer's formal presentation help students to gain mastery of the arts of analysis. The size and format of sections permit more detailed explanation of lecture material by the discussion leader, and allow students to raise questions or objections more readily than in lectures. Lectures present results and leave the student with a clearly defined conceptual universe; discussions search for solutions and enlist students among the seekers. Like the laboratory session or field trip, a section can encourage criticism of the lecturer's assumptions and invite students to go beyond mere assimilation of lecture material to more independent exploration of it. A greater sense of *personal* discovery is possible in a discussion than in a lecture, for the answers emerge as part of a cooperative enterprise, and are not simply stated *ex cathedra*. The section differs from the lab or field trip, however, in that its primary goal is to elicit and compare explanations rather than descriptions, to evaluate rather than to observe. For this reason the sequence—lecture/lab/discussion—forms a pedagogical continuum, each of whose elements enhances the lessons conveyed by the others in an important and distinctive way.

Some small courses are taught through discussion alone. Here, too, the focus is on analysis. How can we prove something to be true? What sort of evidence should we find convincing, and what sort should arouse our suspicions? These questions are the most basic part of any class discussion.[2] Studies of the changes in outlook that students undergo during their four years at college suggest that changes in their pattern of answers are one gauge of their intellectual maturation. Whereas the freshman expects knowledge to be secure and unchanging, as presented in high school textbooks, the senior often has learned to recognize that there may be several "correct" or at least plausible opinions, in addition to others that are clearly fallacious. The delicate balance between rigor and tolerance— applying appropriate standards of proof while recognizing one's ignorance—can be learned in discussion perhaps better than anywhere else. There the teacher offers concrete guidance on how to criticize and how to conduct criticism, just as the lecturer presents the class (most of the time, one hopes) with ideas that compel notice. In both cases, students should be able to absorb a standard of excellence through contact with a teacher.

---

2. See also Chapter Four, "Questioning," by Tom Kazulis, pp. 38–48.

If these are the strengths of the discussion course, then what are its problems? As might be expected, discussions do least well those things that lectures do best. The greatest risk they run is a lack of structure. The meandering conversation, full of intriguing tangents and autobiographical asides, can easily cease to lead anywhere at all. Students used to the definite shape of lectures may become disenchanted with the formlessness of free-association talk fests, and rightly so. Some may need time to appreciate even good discussions. It is up to the discussion leader to explain the rules of the game, to nudge a conversation back on track, to declare some remarks out of order, and generally to keep the peace. It is also incumbent on him or her to relax the fearful students as well as to calm the over-bold. Many undergraduates seek out discussion groups because they feel lost in large lecture courses and want a warm, supportive, friendly atmosphere in which to learn. Some are less able than others to risk censure and criticism from the group, and as a consequence may contribute very little in the end. Yet another problem frequently encountered in discussion groups is the inherently negative bias of the exchanges there. It is far easier to criticize than to construct, and any theory, no matter how promising, leaves room for some objection. If the lecture encourages statements of fact at the expense of criticism, discussions encourage criticism at the expense of positive conclusions. Unless the instructor is careful, the student may come to believe that no generalization truly withstands scrutiny.

Related to the discussion course in method and emphasis are the "tutorial" (as it is called at Harvard) and "independent study." In tutorial one or two, at the most three or four, students meet weekly with a scholar assigned to direct their reading in accordance with their interests and needs. The tutorial is the most flexible tool at the teacher's disposal. The pace of instruction may be adjusted to fit each student far more easily than in a larger group; those who have special aims to pursue may well find them best served here. Few tutorial programs will ever look exactly alike in all details. This places a responsibility on the tutor to discover where the student's interests (and phobias) lie, and how best to deal with both. The tutor is more likely to be aware of how a student's personal problems affect work done in the tutorial, and may feel called upon to address them as well. The student, on the other hand, bears a week-to-week responsibility for her or his assignments that cannot be ignored or postponed with the same ease as in a lecture course. The great strength of tutorial is thus the high level of sustained interaction between two individuals committed to a common educational goal. Students are better able to explore their gifts, and can be helped to overcome weaknesses that might otherwise continue to hamper them. The same could be said of "independent study"—that general category of loosely supervised individual projects—save that here the student is the ultimate architect of success or failure. What the faculty sponsor of an independent project can contribute is encouragement, some bibliographical help, and a practised editorial eye when the time comes to draft a final report. He or she can facilitate the undertaking and certify its quality, but cannot supply what the student is unwilling to give.

What of the informal exchanges between teachers and undergraduates in the library, on the way to class, or over coffee? A suggestion for further reading on a topic of mutual interest, a stated opinion, or even simple encouragement can mean a great deal to a student. The fact that another person takes the trouble to engage the student's ideas seriously helps that student to do the same. Students look to the faculty, not simply for information and approval, but also to learn how certain values are embodied in daily life. Whether or not teachers feel comfortable in this role, they cannot escape being treated as models or exemplars by those younger than they. Good research and good teaching alike involve moral as well as intellectual qualities: honesty, perseverance, self-discipline, service to an ideal. For students, who are maturing emotionally at the same time that they embark on a formal course of study, the message conveyed by a teacher's actions and attitudes may be more instructive than the actual course content.

The final aim of undergraduate education is to make the student independent of the teacher. She or he must ultimately learn to perceive the world, review evidence, form hypotheses, and express conclusions unaided. In a sense, this process appears to be a reversion to the pattern of undirected learning discussed at the beginning of the chapter. But the crucial difference resides in the fact that the student, through exposure to the varieties of teaching available to college undergraduates, has become familiar with a new set of skills and standards. Each type of instruction has its own role to play in creating this final balance. The "structured dialogue" between teacher and student common to all now becomes a silent, inner dialogue where the student acts the teacher's part, offering self-criticism and self-encouragement. The exchange of views and the ability to formulate ideas coherently and forcefully in the presence of others continues to be of prime importance; cooperative learning goes on in boardrooms and government offices and in many other places as a permanent part of professional life. The ultimate authority whose judgment the student should trust and whose counsel he or she should seek, however, lies within. This is the reason why rote learning fails to educate. It does not give the student tools suited for independent use.

A professor of the old school, asked to give his educational philosophy after decades in the classroom, is reported to have said that the matter was really quite simple. It was impossible to have any effect on students at all. "The bright ones will learn no matter who teaches them," he insisted. "The others never will." But the professor was wrong. Teaching does make a difference. It induces students to demand more of themselves, leads them to new ways of solving problems, and awakens unsuspected talents. It can inspire them to become more caring, creative, and thoughtful. But it can only do all this if done well. Poor teaching makes its own kind of difference: it stifles, deadens, and destroys whatever curiosity and enthusiasm students may bring to their studies. And its damage can be permanent.

In order to avoid the pitfalls of poor teaching, teachers themselves must learn to communicate what they know and respond to the needs of their students. Teaching skills, like private student projects, are often assembled at random. The following chapters attempt to do for the teacher what formal instruction does for the student: provide a structure, initiate a dialogue, and propose new standards of excellence and a "sense of style." Teaching, as Gilbert Highet has noted, is an art and not a science. Yet every artist needs a grounding in technique before setting to work, and there is no artist—or teacher—who cannot afford to improve his skill.

CHAPTER TWO

The First Day of Class

Jeffrey Wolcowitz

To students the significance of the first day of classes is clear. During these first meetings, students shop around to learn about the menu of course offerings. There are some sources of information which the student may have consulted already— catalogue descriptions, friends who have taken these courses in the past, and published reports of other people's observations about the course, some reliable and others less so—but they find their personal observations valuable as they wander to the first meetings of far more courses than they will take.

Part of the students' concern is the material that will be covered in the course. One would like to think this is their principal concern when they shop for courses, but we know that they also want to find out what the course requirements are and "to check out the professor." They are looking for as complete a description of the course as possible, including not only the reading list and exam and paper requirements but also the less tangible elements of the course such as the way the class sessions will be conducted, the amount of student-teacher interaction, and the way students will be treated when they raise questions. In a sense students are seeking the terms of the contract they are signing when they enroll in each course.

Instructors generally recognize the importance of providing information about the course for students. Course syllabi take many forms and they vary greatly in the amount of infor-

JEFFREY WOLCOWITZ is Assistant Professor of Economics at Harvard University. He did his undergraduate work at Princeton and his graduate work at Harvard. His research focuses on the layoff incentives of the unemployment insurance tax. From 1978 to 1983 he administered the introductory economics course at Harvard and ran its teaching-training program for new section leaders. He serves on the staff of a workshop on teacher training sponsored by the Joint Council on Economic Education.

mation they contain. Commenting upon this material and making some opening-day remarks about course content and mechanics are often seen by instructors as fulfilling their obligation to tell students what to expect in the course. But the first class meeting also sets the atmosphere for the entire term, so the instructor must begin to establish a framework appropriate to carrying the students from their initial position to achievement of the goals of the course. This requires careful use of the first class hour.[1]

Much of the student-teacher contract that is established or that begins to be established is explicit, written in the course syllabus or stated in class by the instructor. Other parts, those that most often underlie the problems that arise between classes and their instructors later in the term, are implicit. The implicit contract is conveyed through the instructor's attitude and behavior: it feeds into the students' expectations about the way the class will be run, the requirements for being prepared for class, and the sort of relationship this instructor is willing to establish with students. This seems to be what students are trying to learn when they "check out the professor,'' but also what many instructors fail to think about in planning their course. Instructors need to recognize that they are communicating with their students both verbally and nonverbally.

Students are communicating with their instructors on these two levels as well. Effective teaching requires recognizing that the class is composed of individuals, each arriving with a different background and a different set of goals. In order for the instructor to control the learning environment and help students achieve their goals, he or she must learn about the participants in the class. One task of the first day is to collect information about the students by asking them to respond to a series of questions. But the instructor must also begin to read the behavior of the students in order to become sensitive to the individual in the classroom process.

The instructor is responsible for maintaining control of the classroom process not only in a lecture environment but also in an environment where the principal teaching strategy is student-teacher and student-student interaction. An instructor can

---

1. There are a number of details (such as ordering books and checking on classroom space) that teachers will want to pay attention to even before the first day of class. See Chapter Nine, "Learning a New Art," by Richard Fraher, pp. 116–127.

maintain this control and use it to help students learn through careful attention to detail in the classroom and recognition of the importance of nonverbal, as well as verbal, communication. This awareness must begin on the first day in order to achieve the greatest amount possible during the term.

II

A good starting point for the first day of class is stating or writing on the blackboard the title and number of the course and the instructor's name. This provides the lost soul with an opportunity to quietly leave the room unnoticed and it minimizes embarrassment for the instructor who is in the wrong room. Beyond this, the opening segment of the first class must be devoted to a description of the course content and course mechanics, including requirements and operating rules. This is part of the contract which the instructor offers to potential students. It outlines the responsibilities of both parties. Students indicate their acceptance of the contract by enrolling in the course.

The instructor should tell the students as specifically as possible what material will be covered in the course and why. High-flown generalizations about the field might form an exciting lecture but do not help the student choose between this course and other courses. The description should indicate where this course fits in the scope of the field and in the goals of the liberal arts or professional education that the students are pursuing, and must also highlight the specific issues on which the course concentrates. One way of doing this is to go through the syllabus and reading list with the class, explaining the overall organization of the course. A well-constructed syllabus that outlines the major and minor subdivisions serves as a framework for students to organize their thoughts about the course.

In constructing this portion of the opening class, the instructor should try to convey enthusiasm about the course material, as well as provide information. Some instructors offer autobiographical information explaining their own interest in the field—how they became interested, what their particular specialties are, why they find the field exciting. The instructor might also indicate any current relevance of the course material. If the students are excited about the course material from the beginning—feel that it matters or should matter to them—many later problems of weak motivation can be prevented.

Students are very concerned about the workload in the course and tend not to listen to other topics with their full attention until this one is out of the way. Putting together their programs for the term, they recognize their time constraints and try to balance their courses. One aspect of this is the length of the reading list, so a complete reading list should be distributed on the first day. Of even greater importance are the number and timing of exams and papers and the coverage of each. Only with this information and the weights to be assigned to the various parts of the course can students choose a mix of courses that are not *all* difficult and allocate their time effectively during the term. The instructor also benefits from telling students how grades will be computed, as this will reduce the number of inquiries and complaints later in the term. This discussion of requirements and grades should include the instructor's policy for accepting late work so students recognize the cost of getting a late start on assignments or spending too much time on them.

Since students will be using the opening day to decide whether or not to enroll in this course, the instructor should indicate the background she or he will assume that students bring with them. Catalogue descriptions include prerequisites but generally carry the alternative of the instructor's permission. A clear statement of the aspects of the prerequisite courses that the instructor will assume will help students determine whether they will be able to succeed in this course.

Students also want to know how to prepare for class and whether they should come to class if they are not prepared. Students should be told the kinds of questions they should think about in preparing for class. In the case of an introductory course, the instructor should offer some tips on how to study the material, such as the importance of doing problems in math or science courses. If the students will need a special skill, such as "close reading" in a literature course, the instructor should indicate when it will be taught.

Finally, the standard operating procedures of the class should be established. These range from the time at which class will begin to the acceptability of raising questions: will there be times set aside for questions during class or can students raise their hands to ask questions at any time or should all questions be saved for office hours? Students should also be told the extent to which the course will be organized around lectures as opposed to discussion and the special role, if any, that sections

play in the course. If there will be discussion among the students, will the instructor raise questions and wait for volunteers
or will students be called on whether they volunteer or not? Is
it acceptable for students to pass when asked a question? Students should also be informed how their participation will
affect their grades.

What all of these issues have in common is their role in
defining the atmosphere that the instructor would like to create
in the classroom. However, the students will also be drawing
information about the atmosphere of the class from the instructor's behavior. The instructor's actions shape the students'
understanding about what is acceptable behavior in the course
and how the instructor will respond to various situations.

Instructors communicate information about their openness
to students and the formality of the classroom through their
appearance and the way they position themselves in the classroom. An instructor who asks to be called by his or her first
name will be viewed as being more open to interaction with
students than those who insist on being addressed by a title.
Similarly, a graduate student who arrives at class wearing a
three-piece suit will be seen as establishing a greater distance
between himself and his students than one who wears jeans and
a T-shirt to class. Of course, the students' interpretation of this
will differ according to the age and status of the instructor.
What seems appropriate for a graduate student may seem
inappropriate for a full professor. However, it is naive to think
that these aspects do not matter at all.

The instructor's position in the classroom also signals her
or his willingness to entertain student opinions and questions.
A seated instructor imposes less authority than one who is
standing. Remaining fixed behind the podium tends to create
a barrier between the instructor and the class, while by coming
around to the front of the podium, the instructor joins the class
in the consideration of ideas (and gets a student's perspective on
what is written on the blackboard). The optimal position for
the instructor to take will differ between lecture and discussion
courses and among the various classes of the term and the
various parts of the class hour. Part of the art of teaching is the
ability to control and vary the classroom environment through
movement and body language.

Students will generalize from their observations of the
instructor's behavior and will accept these generalizations as the
implicit contract between themselves and the instructor, upon

which they can rely in planning their classroom behavior. The explicit contract is quickly set aside, however, when the implicit contract that is reinforced at each class meeting sets a different standard. Indeed, many of the problems that arise between instructors and their classes later in the term result from the students' adherence to the implicit contract and the instructor's violation of that contract, often in favor of an explicitly stated alternative. Those in a position to hear both student complaints about an instructor and the instructor's own views of the class are often surprised by the inconsistency of these perceptions. The following scenarios illustrate this point:

- *Students complain about the inaccessibility of the instructor while the instructor wonders why no one attends office hours.*
  The instructor may have transmitted indirect signals indicating little interest in the students, perhaps through anger or sarcasm when students ask questions or come to class ill-prepared. No matter how many times such an instructor announces his or her availability at office hours, students may find this instructor unapproachable.
- *An instructor plans to adjust the speed of presentation according to the questions raised by the class, but students claim that questions are not welcome in class.*
  As in the first scenario, this instructor may have appeared annoyed by questions or may have harassed a student who raised one, perhaps refusing to answer or telling the student the answer is "trivial," thus suggesting that anyone who asks a question is stupid. Regardless of the standard operating procedure that the instructor has announced, students in this class will recognize that questions are not welcome.
- *An instructor asks students in class to summarize the reading assignment and finds that no one has read it.*
  An instructor may state that she or he will assume students have done the reading before class, but if the format of the class has not made clear the importance of doing so, students will feel that they can put the reading aside. The class must be structured so that students find the reading necessary to understand the lecture or participate in the discussion.
- *An instructor thinks students are unprepared because no one offers answers to the questions posed in class, but the students have all done the assignment.*

If the instructor answers his or her own questions quickly (perhaps fearing silence) students will view the questions as rhetorical and not offer answers. If the instructor embarrasses a student, a previously lively class can become somber and unresponsive. Calling on a nonvolunteer in class can have similar repercussions if a pattern of choosing only volunteers has been established. By letting the nonvolunteer down gently, an instructor may be able to reduce the damage.

- *A student feels mistreated when the instructor severely reduces the grade on a late assignment.*

  This too may meet the letter of the explicit contract but violate the common law of the implicit contract if the instructor has been lenient in the past about accepting late work. (Accepting late work without a penalty will be viewed as saying that deadlines are not rigid.) Again, the working relationship between the class and the instructor may deteriorate somewhat.

All of these examples are similar in that the instructor is the one who violated the implicit contract, and they were chosen to emphasize that the instructor in the position of control in the classroom must be aware of the contract she or he allows to be established. Of course, students may violate the contract also. Some examples are interrupting speakers in class, turning in late assignments, coming to class unprepared, and calling the instructor at inappropriate times. The instructor must indicate that this is unacceptable either by talking to the student or by grade penalties. Failure to deal with these situations can result in their becoming frequent occurrences in the class or destroying the rapport between the instructor and the rest of the class.

Undoubtedly there are situations in which the instructor realizes that the course is not going as well as he or she would like it to go: what started as a few late problem sets may have become a situation in which no one completes assignments on time; student interaction may have increased to such an extent that the instructor has lost control of the class and cannot progress through the material. This discussion of the implicit contract and the problems that arise from violating it should not be taken to mean that the instructor is faced with an unpleasant choice between maintaining the status quo and alienating the students by blatantly violating the implicit contract.

Rather, a third alternative exists: renegotiating the implicit student-teacher contract by making it explicit. The instructor should acknowledge the problem that has developed and explain why the existing operating procedures are inappropriate to the goals of the class. Explicitly stating the new contract will be viewed by the students as a sign of the instructor's concern for the class and can improve the relationship between the instructor and the students. Of course, only if this new explicit contract is reinforced by consistent behavior will it be taken seriously.

III

Just as students see the first day of class as the time when they learn about the instructor and the way the class will be run, the first class meeting also provides an opportunity for an instructor to begin learning about her or his students. There are two sources of information for the instructor: explicit requests for information and observation of the students' behavior.

People do not agree on what it is fair to know about one's students. At one extreme is the view that students have a right to remain anonymous in class. The justification for this view seems to be a fear that anything an instructor learns about a student will play a role, either consciously or subconsciously, in the grade the instructor assigns to the student at the end of the term. This is indeed a potential problem. In the assignment of grades to papers and exams, we cannot prevent making subjective evaluations. When an answer is somewhat vague, we tend to impute full knowledge to the students we think are smart and less knowledge to those who seem slower. However, it seems that there are other ways to deal, at least partially, with this problem through anonymous grading schemes.

A second argument for student anonymity is that every individual has a right to privacy. Undoubtedly, instructors need to respect this right and display careful judgment in the information they gather about students and the use they make of it. But this right to privacy need not and should not prevent an instructor from gathering information about the individual students that will be helpful in running the class.

In many ways an instructor's view that it is not right to know anything about students except what is revealed in their work for the course is self-serving. Learning about students

requires time and effort. There are many claims on an instructor's time, so anything that can reduce the amount of time
devoted to teaching may appear to be in his or her interest.
However, the failure to learn about the class as a whole and the
individuals who form it acts as an impediment to successful
teaching.

In order to help students learn, instructors need certain
kinds of information about them, in particular what their goals
are, the starting point of their knowledge in the field, and the
constraints that they face in terms of time they can devote to
the course. Students learn best when they are intent on learning; relating new material to the students' accumulated knowledge or current goals helps them recognize the importance of
the topic and increases their interest. Learning involves altering
beliefs and changing thought processes. To be successful in helping students learn, the instructor needs a sense of their beliefs
and modes of analysis at the outset of the course. This allows
a more precise choice of examples, assignments, and discussion
topics to help carry the students from their starting point to the
desired end point. Finally, instructors must recognize that just
as they face other claims on their time, students do not have all
of their time to devote to this specific course.

One might argue that thinking about these issues is part of
the instructor's preparation before the course begins, based on
general information about the entire student population, and
that a self-selection process will lead those students to enroll
who see the course as serving their goals. But particular courses
aid in the pursuit of a variety of student goals and each class
will be different and will respond in different ways. In addition,
the instructor must remember that it is her or his job to control
the flow of class discussion. One must be able to identify key
resource people for various topics, experiences, and perspectives in order to choose who will speak next in the discussion to
keep the class moving in the desired direction. The instructor
should also be sensitive to variations in the behavior of students
over time, in order to avoid interrogating a student at a time of
special stress. The goal, as always, is to help students, not to
hurt them.

Having made this general case for knowing a class and the
individuals who make up the class, we can turn to the more
specific issues of the kinds of information that are useful, ways
of gathering this information, and how it can be used.

At the most basic level, instructors should learn the names of their students. Students generally work harder and respond in a more positive way if they believe the instructor views them as individuals rather than anonymous faces in a crowd. In addition, the instructor's use of names helps students to get to know one another so they may interact in class more easily. While the task of learning names becomes more difficult as class size increases, it is still worth the effort.

There are several things that an instructor might do to make learning names easier. One technique is to have each student fill out an index card giving his or her name (and other information discussed below) and to use these cards as an initial class list for calling the roll and matching faces with names. It is often helpful to use class picture books (generally compiled for the freshman class) to study name-face connections outside the class. Many people have found this speeds up the process of learning names without taking much time, particularly class time, but it is most effective for freshmen because they most resemble their high school pictures. A variation of this is to ask students to provide a recent photograph. Another technique is to ask students who are not called upon by name to identify themselves. Instructors should also use the occasion of returning homework assignments, papers, and exams in class to reinforce the matching of names and faces. In large classes, instructors need to use a seating plan as an aid to learning names.

An index card can be used to collect information as well. In requesting information, the instructor must not compromise the student's right to privacy. At a minimum, the instructor should be able to justify each request for information by explaining how it will be useful in teaching the course, and should be willing to provide similar autobiographical information. The information that will be useful differs from course to course, but several suggestions follow.

- *The student's campus address and phone number.* This is useful if the instructor needs to contact the student during the term, perhaps in regard to an assignment or a student's extended absence from class. The address may also indicate which students are likely to know one another outside of class. The telephone number will be useful if the instructor decides after a class that she or he wants a particular student to discuss an issue in the next class without taking the student by surprise.

- *The student's year in college.* This provides information about the student's assimilation in the college environment and may suggest the constraints on the student's time and the student's commitment to his or her field of concentration.

- *The student's field of concentration.* From this, the instructor gets a sense of the role of this course in the student's academic program. It also provides some indication of the student's background which can be useful in anticipating the way a problem will be attacked.

- *Other courses taken in the field and in related fields.* The student's background in the discipline helps establish his or her familiarity with ideas like those developed in the course and modes of analysis of this field. For courses that take a mathematical approach in a variety of fields, it is useful to know the extent of the student's math background. For a literature course, the instructor might want to know the student's familiarity with the history of the period. This may also indicate to the instructor who the resource people are for certain types of information, the types of examples that are appropriate, and the way individual students might handle a discussion question.

- *Other courses the student is taking that term.* This list suggests the student's time constraints and the relative importance the student places on this course. This is also useful should the student's behavior change during the term, because it allows the instructor to find out whether the student's behavior has changed in other courses as well. This in turn will indicate the extent of the problem and is useful in determining whether the instructor should deal with the problem alone or refer the student to one of the counseling services.

- *Job experience.* Instructors in business courses are particularly interested in this information as they would like to use students as resources in exploring business decisions.

- *The student's home town.* This information indicates which students can be used as resources in a class discussion of a particular example according to their familiarity with the characteristics and problems of various parts of the world.

- *Why the student is taking the course.* The instructor may have some leeway to alter a course in order to meet the specific goals of the students. Alternatively, the instructor might find that the student's reason for taking the course, while a reasonable interpretation of the catalogue description of the course, is really quite different from the instructor's goals in the course. In this case, the instructor can indicate this to the student early in the term and perhaps lead the student to a more appropriate course.

Another source of information about the students in the class is some type of preliminary written exercise. Despite the potential of making students uncomfortable, this can be used successfully if it is ungraded and students understand how it will contribute to the success of the course. One type of exercise is a short diagnostic quiz to indicate to students which parts of the course prerequisites they need to review. In economics, instructors sometimes give quizzes on high school algebra to signal the range of mathematical tools that will be used in the course and then recommend some form of remedial assistance to those who have not done well. Another type of exercise is one which tries to establish the student's starting point in learning the material of the course. In a freshman writing course, for instance, the instructor can assign a short essay to identify each student's particular writing problems in order to adjust the emphasis of the course and to identify particular issues for the students to think about in their first graded assignment. In many courses, it is useful to know the students' prior beliefs about key issues. In economics, before teaching the economic models, an instructor might want to ask students how prices get determined or what causes inflation, using the information to adjust the approach to teaching these concepts.

An alert instructor can learn a great deal about students from their behavior in class. By careful observation, the instructor can learn to "read" her or his class, inferring attitudes of the various individuals and noticing changes in behavior to which she or he should respond. Just as instructors provide information for the students by the way they dress or carry themselves in class, students return similar signals.

One source of information is the student's appearance. A student who consistently wears a tie and jacket to class is more likely to be conservative and espouse conservative views than a gentleman with long hair tied back in a pony tail. In controlling a discussion, the instructor might find it useful to have the conservative point of view brought into the discussion at a certain point. The appearance of the student can be used in deciding which student to choose to make the next contribution to the discussion. Of course, this is not a foolproof method as there are other reasons why students dress the way they do. European students tend to dress more formally than the average American student, regardless of their politics. A student may have a job starting soon after class that requires a coat and tie. Nonetheless, in controlling classroom discussion, the instructor is dealing with probabilities of what given individuals will say at each point of the discussion and these visual signals initially contribute to this information.

Instructors should also be aware of seating patterns in the class. Some students are eager and sit up front. Others are less interested, perhaps taking the course to fulfill a requirement, or shy, and sit near the door. (Of course, a student may also sit near the door simply because he or she has to leave early and does not want to disturb the class.) Students tend to establish seating patterns early in the term and maintain them through the course. Thus, any deviation from this established pattern is a potential source of information. Students may relocate as new friendships develop and groups form, composed of people who prepare for class together. A student may retreat to the back of the room if she or he is unprepared for class, is preoccupied with a personal problem, or is losing the thread of the course. The instructor should avoid calling on these people when they have not volunteered. Lack of sensitivity on the part of the instructor can greatly affect the working relationships that exist in the classroom, not only between the instructor and the student in question, but between the instructor and the entire class: students tend to bond together if one of their cohorts is attacked in a moment of weakness. If a student's unusual behavior persists, the instructor should talk to him or her outside of class.

If possible, the instructor should arrive at class early. This provides a good opportunity to talk informally with students and observe the cultural patterns of the class. Some students will arrive early because they are eager. Others will arrive early carrying a message for the instructor which may never be verbalized, but can be interpreted by an alert instructor. The instructor can observe who arrives with whom and who talks with whom before class. All of these observations help the instructor to make productive use of the resources available in the class.

IV

Having described the goals of the course, paying special attention to the implicit as well as the explicit aspects of the contract being set up with the students and the characteristics of the individuals who make up the class, the instructor is left with the task of beginning to teach the course. The guiding principle in developing a plan for the first lesson should be establishing the standard operating procedure of the class. What gets covered and how it is covered is an important source of information for the students. An actual class provides a more precise and reliable indicator than the instructor's prior description.

In the context of a lecture course it is easy to start establishing a standard operating procedure because there is less reliance on specific preparation and contributions by the students. But even in this context, if the lectures are going to assume careful reading of the assignment before class, this should be made clear by references to concepts that are not developed in the class but covered in the reading.

In discussion courses, there may be a tendency to lecture during the first meeting because students are not prepared to discuss a specific novel or article. While a lecture might be useful if there is a certain body of background information that needs to be transmitted, it gives a wrong signal about the format and should be avoided if possible; reading assignments are often sufficient for providing background facts. One alternative is to use the remaining time as a social occasion. For effective classroom discussion it is important to break down barriers between members of the class and between students and instructors; a social atmosphere can be a good way to achieve this. Another approach is to hand out a brief reading assignment in class, give students a few minutes to read it, and then proceed with a discussion. In a literature course the text may be a poem or a brief essay, while in a social science course this could be a newspaper article or a short case study. For required courses to which students are assigned beforehand, the instructor should consider distributing the reading assignment before the first class meeting. Care should be taken to avoid setting low standards during the first discussion; students should be aware that a quick skimming of the reading assignment is not adequate preparation.

One often hears about instructors who make the first class particularly difficult and intimidating. Once the dust has settled and students have chosen their courses, the instructor moves to a slower pace and reviews in detail the concepts that were assumed or quickly derived in the first class. The goal is probably to generate a small class of high calibre students. This is inappropriate. The wrong signal is being transmitted to students and will result in a poor match between students and the course. The brightest students will be disappointed by the lower level at which the course is actually run and many students interested in the material who have adequate backgrounds for the course will have been scared away. If the instructor feels that the material cannot be taught properly if enrollment is large, it is more appropriate to discuss this with a superior in the department or university, trying to limit enrollment or establish additional sections of the course. If the goal is getting the brightest students it should be recalled that all instructors can try to squeeze out the poorer students, but these students have to go somewhere. The instructor's aim should be a proper matching of students' interests and course offerings.

V

Teaching rests on communication. Human beings communicate both verbally and nonverbally, by their attitudes and behavior. All of these forms of communication are important in the classroom because they help students and the instructor understand one another. These subtle communications begin the first day. Only through careful attention to details and recognition of the human aspects of the process can the instructor gain the control of the classroom that is the prerequisite for learning. While knowledge of students and the particular class process will certainly improve over the course of the term, on the first day the instructor can begin to get her or his message across about the substance and conduct of the course and begin to "read" the class for signs of the students' needs, interests, and expertise.

CHAPTER THREE

The Theory and Practice of Lectures

Heather Dubrow and James Wilkinson

To hear a good lecture is an inspiring experience. We leave with our imagination broadened and our interest piqued; we find ourselves entertained, prodded, and illuminated in turn. What evokes our response is an intricate blend of qualities. The lecture must have sufficient intellectual content to challenge us, and enough clarity of exposition that we are not left disoriented and confused. Like a dramatic monologue, it engages our emotions and keeps them in play, thanks to frequent shifts in mood and intensity. It mixes humor and erudition, and gives us a sense of the personal involvement of the lecturer in his or her topic. It reassures us as well by providing a small island of coherence in an often chaotic world. These elements, taken together, create a series of inner tensions that give life to the lecture. The result may be difficult to define, but is instantly recognizable.

In practice, however, too few lectures attain this ideal. What we find instead is instruction from which one or more essential ingredients are missing, a teaching performance whose good intentions are marred by failures of insight or execution. The industrious but boring lecturer buries students in facts delivered in a monotone, and wonders why the class does not show greater enthusiasm for the material. The energetic but

---

HEATHER DUBROW, who received the B.A. and Ph.D. from Harvard University, is presently Associate Professor of English at Carleton College. The author of *Genre* (Methuen) and a number of articles on sixteenth- and seventeenth-century literature, she is now at work on a study of Shakespeare's non-dramatic poetry.

JAMES WILKINSON's biography is on page 1.

condescending lecturer fires volleys of stirring rhetoric at her or his students yet misses the mark; the students, overawed, are reluctant to seek out an instructor who appears deaf to the opinions of others. The friendly but disorganized professor tells stories of his war service in Burma, leaves half of the course syllabus to cover in the last three lectures, and wonders why the students do so poorly on their exam. Clearly, no teacher should assume that lecturing is an easy business. But much of what distinguishes a good lecture from the less felicitous examples described above can be learned, rehearsed, and perfected. This chapter is intended as a first step toward closing the gap between lecture theory and practice.

Both the virtues of the fine lecture and the faults of the deficient lecture stem from one central fact: the lecturer runs the show. He or she is in charge of what happens during the fifty or so minutes of lecture time far more directly and completely than if this were a discussion class or a tutorial. Such control allows the lecturer to give full play to his or her strengths; wit, eloquence, close reasoning, and gift for entertaining anecdotes need not be suppressed. But control magnifies inadequacies to an alarming degree. The dull lecturer can expect no rescue efforts from the class; the confused lecturer has no escape from tangled thoughts and illegible notes until she or he leaves the podium. The realization of this truth is often enough to cause a severe case of the jitters in even the most self-confident academic.

What can be done to quell such nervousness? The first answer is to plan ahead. Because few allowances need be made for the unknowns that accompany a discussion course—above all the uncertainty as to how long it will take to cover the main points, and in what manner—it is possible to lay out a series of lectures in fairly precise detail. Consider the fundamental questions or themes that the lecture course should explore over the semester, and what their logical sequence should be. Determine how many individual lectures you intend to give, and then roughly block out their content and functional relationship to one another. Even if you teach a survey course in which the topics to be studied seem remote from one another, you should be able to identify broad continuities or contrasts that make sense of the whole. The importance of structure on this general level can hardly be overstressed. It is useless to give your students facts and interpretations, however vivid or stimulating, if you do not at the same time show them how they fit together. A lecture course that lurches from one isolated insight to another without indicating an overall pattern makes it far more difficult to assimilate the material, and far less likely that it will be retained.

This sort of planning requires that you gauge the limits imposed by each lecture. How much can be said in fifty minutes? What sort of unit does a single lecture represent? The answers vary from field to field. But more often than not, novice lecturers try to cover too much ground rather than too little. In some instances, in fact, a good lecture will focus on a single major problem, author, or theorem alone. If it succeeds in doing this, it can be counted a success, provided that links with other lectures are not allowed to disappear from view. One means of drawing attention to such links is through a simple framing device at the start of the lecture. The phrase, "Last time we saw that . . ."—followed by a summary of the foregoing topic—will place the students on familiar terrain, and allow you to show how today's subject proceeds from yesterday's. Another strategy is periodically to devote part of a lecture to the broad view. This may be especially appropriate if you have subdivided the semester's lectures into groups, each focused on one large topic. A course on Victorian fiction, for example, would ordinarily include some lectures on the novels of George Eliot. The first of these might give the students a glimpse of Eliot's growth as an artist and the literary lessons she gained from her predecessors; the last might deal with Eliot's significance for Victorian fiction as a whole.

Once your overall plan is prepared and leaves you feeling reasonably satisfied, then (but only then) comes the time to plan each individual lecture in detail. If the course is new, you may wish to prepare well in advance. If you have given it before, then whatever adjustments the lectures need can be made closer to the time of delivery. How much of a head start you give yourself is largely a matter of personal taste and temperament, however. Some lecturers with a taste for living dangerously write their lectures the night before and find the pressure stimulating; others would find it intolerable. The most common practice for a new course is to complete the bulk of the preparatory reading before the course starts and then to keep about a week ahead. What sources you consult when preparing each lecture will clearly be determined by your subject. In some cases you will confront primary texts, in others you will find yourself heavily dependent on secondary literature. Unlike a book or an article, a lecture can be brought continually up to date, receiving fresh transfusions of ideas from either your own ongoing research or recent scholarship. The best idea is to designate a certain number of old lectures—perhaps as many as a third—for special attention and revision each year, while you tinker with the others as time allows.

Lectures provide the scaffolding without which the course would collapse. But in addition, there are assigned readings for the students and perhaps section meetings as well. How should readings and sections be integrated with your lectures? Do not assume that your students will keep pace with the lecture material as they read; most will fall behind at some point, and a few will lag from the very beginning. The course syllabus should make clear in what order and by what date the assigned readings are to be completed. Your job as lecturer, however, is to introduce the books or articles on your reading list as they come along and whet the students' appetite, if possible, by explaining their value and significance. Like the author of a good preface, you should be informative without presuming that your audience is familiar with the work. When the material is unusually difficult, part of the lecture can be given to illuminating the dark corners of the text in a systematic way. Readings and lectures, that is to say, should at all times complement one another. Nothing so irritates students as a course whose reading assignments are completely divorced from the lecture topics. But neither should lectures simply repeat what the students are required to read on their own. Those lectures on George Eliot, if they do not do more than simply rehearse the plot and characters of *Adam Bede* or *Middlemarch,* will prove a bore for all concerned.

Sections, too, should complement the lectures rather than duplicate them in any significant fashion. Here difficult topics can be discussed in greater detail, alternative questions fielded and opinions solicited. Despite their flexible character, sections should be planned in advance with as much care as you give to the lecture schedule. If you have course assistants or teaching fellows who are responsible for conducting some of the sections, it is essential that you hold a strategy session with them before each section meeting, both to indicate what you expect to be done and to hear their suggestions. A special section close to exam time will usually be much appreciated by the students, for it is then that many of their questions will suddenly emerge as they reread old lecture notes and try to put the course in order.

The close interdependence among lecturer, readings, and sections imposes a cardinal requirement on the lecturer: do not fall too far behind. However strong the temptation, do not spend six class hours discussing that favorite theory of yours when you had planned to spend only three. Don't decide that Kant really deserves half the semester when you had originally allotted him a week. The course description in the catalogue and the course syllabus that you distribute to your students at the first class each constitute a promise of intent. You cannot disregard your part of the bargain and expect the students to remain oblivious or unconcerned. Some adjustments may be necessary as the semester progresses, especially if you discover that the class is experiencing real difficulty in learning material you assumed would be easily grasped. But always try to work within your overall lecture plan. Use sections to help those in difficulty, or office hours, or a part of a lecture now and then. Don't lose sight of your final destination, whatever happens.

Just as the key to a good discussion is skillful questioning by the discussion leader, the key to a good lecture is delivery. All the preparation in the world will not by itself ensure a successful course; the expert who cannot communicate what he or she knows is useless as a teacher, for the art of teaching is to help others understand by making your knowledge accessible. Fortunately, there is a remedy at hand. The first step, once again, is to chart your itinerary. "Before he opens his mouth," Gilbert Highet writes, "the lecturer must know exactly what points he wishes to tell his audience, in what order, and with what emphasis." For all but the most experienced and most accomplished, Highet's prescription means that the lecturer must come equipped with notes. These need not be a verbatim text of what she or he intends to say. A detailed outline, with the major points and transitions between them set out legibly, is all that is really required. Ten pages of typed, single-spaced notes, including quotations written out in full, is generally a maximum of what you can use in one fifty-minute lecture. Many lecturers make do with less. Others, however, write out the entire lecture, or append a written first paragraph to the notes that follow. Suit yourself.

No matter what your choice, you should strive for a delivery that is as lively and engaging as possible. Those who prefer notes to an elaborate manuscript find that notes encourage inventiveness and spontaneity. Reading makes for a more polished lecture, but may also invite dullness. You are not really thinking, nor are you likely to be paying attention to the mood of your audience; instead, you are turning printed symbols into sounds. Therefore take care to read with inflection and expressiveness. But whichever approach you use, vary your speed, speaking slowly and emphatically when you come to an important point, relaxing and picking up the delivery when you move on. Under no circumstance should you speak as rapidly as you would in a normal conversation, since students need time to have your words sink in. If this seems strange at first, try mimicking the delivery speed of a news broadcaster on radio or television. You will discover that he or she is speaking much more slowly than you imagined.

Delivery is not simply a matter of planning and inflection, however. It demands variety and balance as well. In order to hold your students' attention, you must alternate between general information and detail, difficult concepts and easy ones, gravity and humor. You can overdo the use of any; the trick is to keep all in proportion. The most effective way to do this requires that you develop a sense for the rhythm of student reactions over the course of a normal fifty-minute lecture. Here, as in writing, the first rule is: start well and end well. The initial ten minutes and final five minutes deserve special attention, since that is when students will be most receptive to your message. One of the best ways to put this time to good effect is to begin with a problem, and end with a solution. During the thirty-five intervening minutes you can present the logical steps and illustrative material leading from one to the other, being especially careful to watch for signs of students' boredom about halfway through the lecture. This is the dead point for most audiences; if you have any entertaining stories that relate to your argument, tell them now.

The teacher has some other aids for keeping student attention besides her or his own voice. Gestures can serve to underline a point quite effectively. One Harvard lecturer of note used to pace back and forth on the podium, trailing his microphone cord behind him, and reverse direction at the end of each sentence, punctuating it with a snap of the cord. For the less flamboyant, there are also the teacher's old friends, blackboard and chalk. A lecture that involves unfamiliar terms, dates, or names can be made more accessible to the students if this information is placed on the board at the start of the hour. Some teachers go further and outline the lecture at the same time. Others prefer to put up diagrams or short sentences as they go along. For lectures in the sciences, the blackboard is indispensable, and may at times almost supplant the lecture itself as the principal agent of instruction. The two rules to remember when using the blackboard are to be sure that you are speaking audibly when your back is to the class, and that everyone has copied what seems pertinent from the board before you erase it.

Other valuable aids include slides and films. Slides are easier to integrate into a lecture, since you can continue talking with a picture on the screen, and make your points referring to it as you would to the blackboard. For some subjects such as field biology or fine arts, it is difficult to conceive how one could teach properly *without* slides. A common mistake that lecturers make when first showing slides, however, is to misjudge how many they will need. Here it pays to consult an experienced practitioner, since the norm varies according to the topic. Two dozen slides of Rembrandt paintings will be too many if you devote much time to each; if you are discussing fern species, you may want twice that number. Films, especially short ones, can also be a great help in some courses. Developmental psychology and cultural anthropology are two fields that lend themselves especially well to teaching through film. If the film is a good one, it will of course overshadow your lecture, and you should be prepared to base your remarks as much as possible on the film in order to exploit its full effect. Both slides and films demand projection equipment that functions without a hitch. Check beforehand to make sure that you or someone else knows how to operate the relevant machines; otherwise your class will rapidly tune out.

The physical setting of a lecture course affects both lecturer and students. Adequate lighting, easy access to a blackboard, public address equipment, comfortable seating all help a great deal. Unfortunately, there may be little you can do if these or other amenities are lacking. The best course of action is always to visit the lecture room before your first class begins, try out a few remarks on some imaginary students, and see how you feel. Perhaps you will discover some adjustments you want to make in your normal routine; at least you will know where the light switch is when the time comes to use it later on. Once the lecture course is underway, you may find that the class size itself affects your delivery. If you are used to lecturing to only thirty students and suddenly face three hundred, your tone and gestures will have to become more deliberate and sharply defined. Concentrate on projection. If your class is smaller than you anticipated, you can afford to relax and become more informal. Over time, you will probably develop a variety of lecture styles to meet a variety of demands. As Laura Nash suggests in Chapter Six, the process of adopting a public *persona* before the class is both unavoidable and salutary. But the best lecturers retain as much of their personality and natural manner as possible in every teaching situation.

There are few lecturers who have not asked themselves, looking out at a sea of expectant faces, just what the students want from them. Clearly, different students expect different things; no one approach will please all. Teachers whom beginning students find helpful because their lectures are straightforward and undemanding may appear dull to those more advanced. The best the lecturer can do is to try to gauge the needs of the majority, and try to help the others after class or in section. But there remain a few basic student expectations, commonly shared, that no lecturer should ignore. A surprising number of students, when asked, will regularly say that what they value most in a lecture is enthusiasm. As one undergraduate put it, "I always wonder what makes a professor devote his life to scholarship—watching a lecturer get really turned on by his material helps me understand." Not only does enthusiasm convince students of your love for the subject; it can be contagious as well. Members of the class are more likely to do the course reading (and much more likely to do it as the term progresses, rather than the night before the exam) if they get the sense that this is exciting stuff. The converse is also true. If you find the material boring, so will they.

Students prize clarity no less than intellectual passion. They like a well-ordered course for aesthetic reasons, perhaps, but certainly on the very practical grounds that clarity facilitates retention. Many students walk into a lecture genuinely concerned about taking good notes. They realize that summaries of lectures will be essential in studying the material later on; often, too, they interpret the contents of their notebooks not only as a source but also as a symbol of what they have learned, believing that records that are both copious and comprehensible prove the course's value. Other students who are struggling to keep up will find their task yet more difficult if the lectures do not lend themselves to easy transcription. The moral is obvious: help your students to take good notes by anticipating their needs. Repeat important points, stress logical interconnections. prepare them for what you are about to say, speak slowly. If you see students in class who are writing down little or nothing to try to find out why. It may be that the problem is not the material, but you.

Another type of expectation, however, may well be less legitimate and hence frequently poses problems for lecturers. Students often assume that what they hear in a lecture is simply and indisputably true. Some, of course, are still accustomed to accepting the authority of the teacher without question and believing that her or his most casual thoughts are invariably pearls of wisdom. But even students who enjoy the complexities and ambiguities they encounter in discussion groups often expect that lecturers will provide not tantalizing problems but rather tidy solutions, not educated guesses but rather distilled truth. The physical settings of many lectures, with a raised podium placed at some distance from the audience, readily support these students' expectations. Such presuppositions about the nature of the lecture are less likely to be a problem in more advanced courses, although even there certain students will be prone to misinterpret a tentative theory as a well established truth. The lecturer's sole recourse is to present conflicting opinions and hypotheses wherever appropriate, and to stress that no one approach is immune from criticism.

A teacher who does this conscientiously will inevitably encourage questions from the floor. How are they to be handled? The answer depends on your sense of how widely the question is shared. If the point raised would seem of interest to many students, then there is a good case for taking time from the lecture and exploring it on the spot. If, on the other hand, the question strikes you as narrow or decidedly offbeat, then an answer is better saved for after class. Simply tell the student that he or she should come up to see you once the lecture is over, and that you will explore the topic with them at that time. Never make the student feel that the question is a foolish one. Critical faculties all too frequently tend to be dulled by prolonged sitting and note-taking; an active response to your lecture, as long as it does not disrupt or distract the class as a whole, should be welcome.

There are many other kinds of student response while the lecture is in progress, and all provide useful information to the lecturer. You can actually see a great deal from where you stand on the podium, especially if you lift your head from the lecture notes now and then. Use this contact to monitor your progress. What you hope to observe is a class with their attention riveted on you, the lecturer. If your audience is motionless (save for hands employed in energetic transcription of the lecture) then you have them with you, and all is well. Yawns, fidgeting, staring out of the window are all obvious trouble signs; the more restless the class, the more bored it is. What can you do to calm squirming students? The best tactic is to move on quickly to your next substantive point, thereby hoping to regain their attention, and at the same time to check your delivery by going down a short mental list. Are you speaking audibly? Slowly enough? With enough emphasis? Try varying your delivery somewhat and see if the squirming abates. Although some classes will tell you when you cannot be heard (shouts of "Louder!" from the rear of the hall), few if any will tell you outright that they find you dull and uninspiring. That message they reserve for body language.

There are times in a lecture course when something goes seriously wrong and you find yourself forced to react on the spot. If you make a slip of the tongue or a computational error that elicits laughter or hisses, correct the error (apologize if need be) and move on. If you don't know what you have said to elicit the response, ask. If the lights go out or the pipes begin to bang, send someone for the janitor and explain to the class that you have done so. If your problem is an openly disruptive student or students, however, then you are going to have to show some diplomatic flair. In general, the class will side with you and against the rowdy types as long as you act in a civil manner and do not overplay your authority. To give a little, and then be firm but polite is the best rule. If there are some things you prefer not to have going on in your classroom—

whispering, late arrivals, newspaper reading—say so. Your section leaders, placed strategically around the lecture hall, can often keep these activities from getting out of hand. But remember, there are limits to what you and they can accomplish; nuisances of a minor nature you must learn to tolerate.

Some of the most important types of learning that take place in a lecture course do not necessarily occur during the actual lectures themselves. The teacher may use less formal contacts with students to clarify points, to encourage extra reading, and even to counterbalance the passivity that, as we know, listening to lectures too often breeds. One of the simplest and most effective ways to encourage students to think through the material of the course—and to remove what is so often a barrier to such thinking, an undue sense of distance from and even awe toward the lecturer—is simply to be accessible whenever possible for casual conversations before and after class. Students who are shy about coming in to office hours are often willing, even eager, to talk informally in the classroom itself. They may also respond to indirect signals that the lecturer is happy to chat with members of the class more readily than they do to an overt invitation. If, for example, you step down from the stage immediately after the lecture and linger a bit, students who otherwise might hesitate to do so will often come up to ask questions or just talk about the course.

Office hours assume an especially important role when the lectures are not supplemented by discussion classes. Adding a couple of extra hours during the weeks when students are most likely to need help, such as at the beginning of the term and immediately before exams, is a much appreciated gesture. Students who are having trouble in a course often become entangled in a vicious cycle, especially if they do not have a sympathetic section leader (or any section leader at all) to whom they can turn. The difficulty they are having in following the lectures, doing the reading, or in completing written assignments leads them to avoid doing other work for the course, which in turn encourages them to stop coming to lectures, which in turn makes it even harder, practically and emotionally, for them to catch up. One obvious but important way to counter this pattern is to encourage students to come in to your office hours (or to see their section leader) as soon as a problem arises, rather than waiting until it gets out of hand. If you find members of the class slipping behind, call them or send a note asking to see them. But even students who are in good standing and do not wish to take advantage of office hours will be pleased to know you are there; your availability is read as a sign that you care.

Students generally welcome review sessions shortly before exams. It can be useful to think beforehand about which topics you might wish to repeat or enlarge on, since questions are occasionally slow in getting started. One format that works well is to begin with a general description of the exam (how many essay questions, how many spot passages or identifications, how heavily it will count) and then to offer practical advice about studying. Even the brightest students have sometimes failed to master efficient study habits. They, no less than others, may benefit from the observation that many people remember best the material that they review immediately before bedtime, or the suggestion that studying in groups may prove particularly helpful given the subject matter of the course. Once you have given the class general advice, try to let them see what sort of answers you expect, and what sort you would rather have them avoid. It is sometimes possible to pass out a sample essay, with comments and corrections, that will show them your standards in a very direct fashion. Then you can turn to the more difficult aspects of the course so far, offer suggestions for coping, and finally solicit questions from the floor.

The feedback you get back from your students throughout the term can be quite as informative to you as the advice you bestow on them during review sessions. Many teachers choose to supplement whatever official evaluation (if any) the university may provide at the end of the term with a more informal questionnaire or even, if the lecture class is small enough, a discussion of the course around the middle of the semester. This procedure makes it possible to take the students' suggestions into account while they are still around to benefit; many undergraduates really appreciate this sign that the teacher is concerned with their reactions. Like so many other proofs of good will on the teacher's part, it carries with it the indirect benefit of encouraging members of the group to devote themselves to the course with enthusiasm.

Useful though the students' reactions may be, they are, of course, only one of the many ways you have to evaluate the quality of your lectures. Arranging with a colleague to sit in on each other's classes can be illuminating (and less threatening than it may sound). The styles even of teachers espousing very similar pedagogical principles can differ dramatically, so you can often pick up new ideas by watching someone else lecture, as well as benefit from their comments on your own presentation. Videotaping lectures is also both infinitely more informative and substantially less intimidating than one might at first suppose.[1] Many of the mannerisms that can annoy an audience show up clearly on tapes; we are often totally unaware of, say, a habit of frowning at a dramatic moment in the lecture. Recognizing such patterns of behavior is half the battle. Once we acknowledge their existence, mannerisms often disappear on their own.

Watching a tape may remind us once again how many different components contribute to a good lecture—the content, the physical bearing of the lecturer, timing, humor, and delivery. But the very fact that so many elements interact during a lecture is not only a reminder of how many things can go wrong, but also a reminder of how many ways we have to cure or at least to compensate for limitations as lecturers. Someone who is conscious of having a high and reedy voice may, for example, work on modulating it, while at the same time counterbalancing it by standing closer to the audience or adding dramatic pauses to a lecture. Equally important is to discover the things you do well, and build your delivery around them. Literature teachers with a gift for reading verse, for instance, may well choose to do so more frequently than some of their colleagues.

If lecturing is, as this chapter has suggested, a fine art and a difficult one, it can also be very enjoyable. And you will be at your best when you feel the pleasure affecting your lecture style. Enthusiasm for the process of lecturing communicates itself just as readily as your enthusiasm for your subject matter. Despite some residual nervousness, despite the hurried breakfast spent poring over your notes and last-minute worries over whether you have enough to say, you can still step up to the podium and honestly tell yourself: "This is going to be fun."

---

1. The process of videotaping is described more fully in Chapter Nine, "Learning a New Art," by Richard Fraher, pp. 116–127.

CHAPTER FOUR

Questioning

Thomas P. Kasulis

It is the night before the new instructor's first discussion class. She has looked through the reading assignment one last time, has outlined the central points to be covered in class, and has checked some (if only there were more time!) of the relevant secondary materials. She is better prepared than she ever was for any class as a student. She is tired, but as she prepares to turn in for the night, she mulls over the last detail. "What questions should I ask so that we will cover the material in the most interesting and educational manner?" Suddenly she realizes she is stumped. What if the students don't respond to her questions? What if there is just silence? She feels an anticipatory twinge of nausea. Her head feels dull and hollow; her mouth dry. For twenty years of formal education, she has been the one who answered the teacher's questions in the classroom. Suddenly tomorrow morning at nine o'clock she will be the one who asks the questions. And if the questions fail, the class fails; if the class fails, she fails.

Most college teachers were once good students, even stars, in their discussion classes. It is natural, then, that a new teacher would tend to stay with the pattern of class preparation that had always proven so successful as a student: the meticulous reading of the assignment, the determination of key points likely to come up in class and a listing of possible questions

THOMAS P. KASULIS, 1979–80 Harvard Mellon Faculty Fellow, received his B.A., M.Phil., and Ph.D. in Philosphy from Yale, and an M.A. in Asian Philosophy from the University of Hawaii. He taught at the University of Hawaii for five years and is currently the Chairman of the Department of Philosophy and Religion at Northland College. His areas of specialization are Asian thought, modern Continental philosophy, and comparative philosophy of religions. His book, *Zen Action/Zen Person*, was published by the University Press of Hawaii in 1981.

to raise should the opportunity present itself. As our anecdote implies, however, teaching a discussion class is different from being a student in one. The crux of the difference will be explained in terms of questioning.

I
Three Dimensions of Discussion

When a student asks a question, it is almost always directed to the content of the class, that is, to what the course is about. This is only one dimension of a classroom discussion, however, albeit the most obvious to the student. A teacher's question is often more complex in its intention—the teacher may wish not only to raise a certain issue, but also to change the tempo of the discussion or to involve a quiet student in the dialogue. In other words, the teacher must be aware of, and responsible for, all three interrelated dimensions: the content (what the class is about), the process (how the class is functioning) and the persons (who is involved in the class). Let us briefly consider each.

Content is the most obvious facet of the seminar or discussion section and only a most irresponsible teacher would fail to give it due consideration. In fact, if anything, the new instructor is often *too* well prepared in terms of content. What new teacher has not zealously written up reams of notes, checked supplementary readings, worked out a lesson plan of things to be discussed—only to find that the actual class could cover but a tenth of the material? This enthusiasm for content is not accidental: one's entrance into graduate school depended on it and graduate training itself concentrates almost exclusively on content. So graduate students-turned-instructors naturally fall into the trap of overemphasizing content, with its risk of neglecting students' legitimate learning needs.

A class is also a *process,* an independent organism with its own goal and dynamics. It is always something more than what even the most imaginative lesson plan can predict. The metaphors are revealing. How often have we heard someone say that the discussion "ran away from us" and the teacher had to step in to "kill" it? The teacher is responsible for not only what is discussed, but also how it is discussed. Are the students involved or just going through the paces? Do some students dominate others? Is the class too sedate or too argumentative? Is there a tendency for the discussion to wander off into empty abstractions or to muddle around in the anecdotal? Such concerns reflect the process of student-student and student-instructor interactions.

Since instructors are responsible for the interactions of the seminar or discussion section, they should be as conscientious in preparing for the class's process as for its content. How does one prepare for process? One technique is to have a process plan to accompany the lesson plan. As one considers which issues should be covered first and which later, one should give forethought to *how* each issue should be discussed. For the first point in today's class, would one prefer dialectical controversy or group consensus building? For the next topic, would one like to encourage a free exchange of ideas or an analytic, systematic approach? Often teachers know quite well that their classes tend to be lively but superficial, or critical but ponderous. By developing a process plan, the instructor can try strategies for creating a more satisfactory balance. Later, we will discuss specific techniques by which one can direct the process plan through questioning, but our point here is that one must first have a plan. Like the lesson plan, a process plan should be flexible and should foresee alternative routes to the same general goal. One should even be willing to abandon the plan entirely if something unexpected but valuable has spontaneously taken form. But it is better to have a plan that can be adjusted or ignored than to have no plan at all.

A discussion is not only the process of collectively examining a set of issues; it is also the *persons* involved in that task. Any instructor who has taught multiple sections of the same course will attest to the fact that no two classes are ever the same. To prepare for a class discussion without taking into consideration the personalities, strengths, and needs of the people in the course is to depersonalize teaching. It is to teach the course and not the students. Although the content of a course may be the same from section to section or from year to year, each class has its own character and deserves recognition of that fact.

The problem again is how to prepare for this dimension of the discussion. The instructor should know how each student operates in the classroom. Which students are fast thinkers and which more deliberate? Who is most comfortable with abstractions and who can best connect the abstract with the concrete? Which student commands the most attention from the class? Whose comments are most often ignored? Who is the best listener? What are the class alliances: talkers *vs.* nontalkers? theoreticians *vs.* empiricists? males *vs.* females? majors *vs.* nonmajors? The more fully these questions can be answered, the more skillful the teacher can be in directing a fruitful discussion. If the class has become dry and theoretical, for instance, the teacher may interject, "How would this theory apply to today's political scene?" Three students may raise their hands: one may intend to bring the discussion back to the theoretical; another to take it to the level of practical politics; another may want to introduce a Marxist slant. Without permanently stereotyping students, the teacher can try to anticipate students' responses. The more this can be done, the more the discussion can be controlled merely by calling on the right person at the right time.

A good way to sensitize oneself to the personal dimension is to keep a brief record or diary at the end of each class session detailing such points as who spoke when, what was said, and who responded to whose point. At first it is difficult to remember the details, but this is often a sign that one has not been adequately aware of human dimensions during the class. After a few sessions, however, one will be able to anticipate which students will give which kind of response. Seeing the students as individuals, the teacher can call on a student at the interesting moment when that individual's perspective would be most relevant to the progress of the discussion. As the individuality of each student becomes recognized, the students will learn to listen to, and respect, one another's comments.

Should the instructor call on nonvolunteers? Whatever one decides, it is important to be consistent. The advantage of calling on nonvolunteers is naturally that it involves all students in the discussion. Its disadvantage is that it may provoke anxiety in the more reticent or shy student. One strategy is to distribute before each class a few study questions for which the students will be responsible. Then with respect to those questions at least, the teacher is entitled to call on any student. Using such a format, the teacher may opt to start a class by calling on a student who did not speak during the last session, for example.

If the teacher does decide to call on only those who have raised their hands, the teacher must learn to *wait*. One does not have to call on the first person who volunteers, nor the second, nor the third. In fact, one may have to wait a few moments until the more deliberate thinkers have the chance to formulate their answers. By his or her actions, the instructor must show that replies do not have to be quickly formulated in order to be welcomed and discussed. Similarly, the teacher should not be embarrassed to wait if there are no immediate volunteers to answer a question. Often it takes time to think through a response. Both the teacher and students should appreciate that. Furthermore, the teacher can be cognizant of subtle signs of a student's desire to participate—a look in the eye or a shifting in the seat, perhaps. Sometimes in such cases the teacher's glance in the student's direction is enough encouragement so that the hand will go up.

II
Three-Dimensional Questioning

The discussion leader's primary tool is the question. For a question to be effective, it must ask about the right issue, at the right time, of the right person. Suppose, for instance, that Mary has just made a comment about Kant and one would like her to expand on it. If the class dynamics have been satisfactory and Mary's participation in the class unproblematic, then one might simply ask, "Mary, could you elaborate on that point a little further?" Suppose, however, the class process has been such that the teacher would like to increase the student-student interaction. One might say in that case, "Mary, could you relate that to what John was saying earlier about Kant?" Now it may well be that Mary did not really listen to what John had said, and the teacher might have to help a bit at first. But if one starts asking questions that require students to respond to each other, they will become more attentive. Similarly, if the class has fallen into a sedate relativism in which no one cares to examine anyone else's view critically, the teacher might try to force a confrontation by asking, "Then you don't accept the interpretation John just gave?" (Incidentally, to increase confrontation, ask questions of people sitting across the room from each other; to decrease it, ask questions of people along the same side. It is easier to argue with someone whom you face at a distance.) Suppose, however, that the class process has been going as planned, but the teacher is concerned that Mary, one of the best writers in the class, has been hesitant to express her views in the seminar. Say, for example, she wrote a strong paper on empiricism and she knows the teacher thought highly of it. Then one might personalize the question in the following form, " Mary, you're sounding like an empiricist again. What do you think an empiricist might say to Kant's argument?"

Thus, questions can function in all three dimensions of discussion and the skillful teacher can pose questions that develop all three areas. Without devising any complex typology, let us briefly examine some of the ways in which this can be done.

In terms of content, questions may elicit a factual or an interpretive response: that is, a question may ask for a straightforward answer ("How many of Thomas's proofs for the existence of God begin with an empirical generalization?") or for an arguable one ("Which of Thomas's proofs is the strongest?"). The proportion between these two types of questions will vary with the discipline: there are likely to be more factual questions in a chemistry class than in a literature class, for example. In any case, however, factual questions can have an important function. First, they clarify for the student what the starting point of any interpretation must be—facts. Second, they may work well as warm-ups for more complex and abstract questions. Third, they are relatively unthreatening and so may be a way of involving a well-prepared, but shy, student in the discussion.

An interpretive question, on the other hand, requires the respondent to go beyond the letter of the text in order to relate, criticize, clarify, justify, extrapolate, or apply the ideas under discussion. In short, factual questions require mainly the classification of information and its retrieval; interpretive questions require evaluation and synthesis. The requested interpretation may be either specific or general. Specific interpretive questions ("Why does Thomas appeal to empirical experience in his proofs?") are more directive. Hence, they reveal some of the standpoint and lesson plan of the teacher. General interpretive questions ("Why does Thomas use the kind of arguments he does?") are more open-ended and elicit the varied concerns and perspectives of the entire group. Any effective discussion will move back and forth between the two levels. If all the questions are on the general plane, the discussion will lose its continuity. If all the questions are specific, the students may feel the discussion is manipulative; that is, the teacher is making her or his own statement by asking a long series of leading questions. This often results in the famous student preface, "I don't know if this is what you are looking for, but. . . ."

One strategy for avoiding the overuse of leading questions is simply to distribute a set of such questions to the students ahead of time. Then they will be able to study the material with that line of thought in mind and will come to class ready to *start* from there. The "manipulative questions" have thereby been transformed into useful "study cues." For the teacher, this means the students will cover material at home that formerly had to be handled in class. This allows more time for open-ended discussion.

There are at least five ways in which questions can be specifically designed to accomplish a change in the discussion process. First, a question may be intended to create a break, to start over, or to mark the transition from one point of the discussion to the next. From my own college days, I recall a professor whizzing us through a proof in mathematical analysis, then stopping, turning to his gaping, awestruck undergraduates and saying, "That was proof one. James, what shall we call the next?" "Proof two?" "Excellent, James. You show promise for doing advanced work in number theory." Obviously, the question was purely rhetorical. It was not intended to teach us anything at all. But it did return us to square one, giving us a chance to catch our breath before a new assault. Similarly, simple factual questions can be used as a quick review of where the discussion has gone, as an ice-breaker at the beginning of a class, or as a tempo quickener when the class has drifted off into the doldrums. A series of short, quickly answered questions that are not too simple tends to make the class more alert and ready to tackle more difficult issues. Such questions are, in fact, almost purely within the dimension of process. Their purpose is not really to elicit information, but rather, to accomplish something in the classroom dynamics.

A second way a question can facilitate the process of discussion is by including a specific qualifying instruction with it, such as, "In a few words . . ." or "If you had to pick just one theme. . . ." Such questions are obviously designed to elicit something other than a definitive analysis. They set a lively tempo for the discussion and establish a cornerstone on which the class can build. Sometimes they may mitigate the fear of criticism, since everyone recognizes that any brief answer is likely to be flawed in some respects. Questions with built-in limits are very effective in bridling the loquacious and in getting several students involved in the discussion within a few minutes.

A third way questions serve process is in giving an instruction as to level of abstraction, as in, "If you were to generalize . . ." or "Can you give some specific examples?" Such a question may radically alter the energy level of a discussion. If the class has become cerebral and abstract, for instance, one may want to bring it back to the concrete. If it is heated and explosive, one may want to talk in terms of general principles, something less volatile than the too real particulars. There is no universal rule about whether it is better to start with the specific and move to the general or vice versa. The sudden transition from one level to the other does have an important impact on the classroom dynamics, however, and skillful teachers use sudden transitions to create a shift in the mood or learning process of the class.

A fourth way questions may serve process is by making reference to other students' comments, such as, "Harry, would you tend to agree with Rick on this point?" (As noted above, this type of question increases student-student interaction.) Furthermore, it can be used to emphasize an earlier point that was not fully appreciated by the class at the time. If the teacher refers back to Rick's earlier comment, for example, students infer that it was somehow important. This is a less obvious technique than having the teacher say, "Rick made a good point earlier. Let us go back to it now."

Finally, a question may be used to elicit a summary or give closure, as in, "Jennifer, if you had to pick two or three themes that recurred most often in our discussion today, what would they be?" This is obviously a very difficult kind of question to ask a student and one must be cautious with it. Some students, however, can summarize very well. If the teacher can discover who those students are, their special skills can be utilized. This again would avoid the entrance of the teacher as a *deus ex machina* who appears at the end of the class to resolve all problems and tell us what is important.

In terms of the third dimension of the classroom discussion, questions can also be directed in such a way that they make the educational experience more personal or individualized. One of the great lessons to be learned from a discussion class is that there is more than one valid way to approach a question. One strategy for accomplishing this goal is to help the individual students understand their own approaches vis-à-vis others'. When a student has been working toward a per-

sonal articulation of a given standpoint, the teacher may refer
to that standpoint in the class discussion. For example, John
may be most interested in the aesthetic aspects of Japanese
thought, whereas Betty may be intrigued by the political. By
referring to these interests in the questions raised in class, the
teacher alerts the students to their own similarities and differences. Eventually, the students may direct some of their classroom questions to a fellow student when the issues relate to
that person's particular interest—they may even argue and carry
the discussion for a while on their own.

What distinguishes a personalized question from a personal
question? What information about a student may the teacher
share with the class? Obviously, it is all right to ask Henry about
his major, but it would be inappropriate to ask him about his
feelings for his father unless Henry himself brought up the subject in class for some relevant reason. The point is to create a
classroom environment in which students will recognize each
other as individuals, but will also feel no pressure to reveal
their private lives. By designing questions which relate what
Kathy said last week to what she is saying now, or relate what
Jerry and Mark both said today, the teacher can personalize
and enrich the class without invading the students' privacy.

III
Actually Teaching

Let us return to the story which opened this chapter.
Suppose now that our protagonist has managed to work through
her despair by coming to the same conclusions we have reached.
She has prepared a process plan, has learned what she can about
the students, and will compile a record of the class after it is
over.

*She has asked her opening questions and the responses are
good. The class is only a few minutes old, but already she is into
the thick of it. Hands are going up, questions are being raised.
She is making mental notes about content, process and per-
sonnel: "Marv tends to be long-winded so I'd better use limita-
tion questions with him. The student-student interaction is
nil; I'll use more personalized questioning. Bill (or is it Jack?)
looks bored and sleepy. Beth likes to talk in abstract terms.
Meg (Martha?) . . . Wait, what did Jim just say? The main theme
of the* Myth of Sisyphus *is what? Whose turn is it now? This is*

*going too fast!" She is hesitating now. A quiver in the voice,
moisture on the palms. Her pulse is getting faster and faster.*

We cannot leave our topic without making the transition
from the rarefied ideal to the flesh-and-blood reality. Our
theory requires the teacher to be simultaneously aware of three
dimensions. In practice this is impossible. Teaching is not
simply an intellectual exercise. In fact, it is closer to playing
a sport than solving a geometry problem. This should be obvious, but it is often overlooked. The actual teacher in the classroom is looking one student in the eye and listening to what she
or he is saying, but is also peripherally aware of a hand being
raised on the other side of the room. People are gesturing;
diagrams are written on the blackboard; the teacher's voice is
an instrument to speed up or slow down the tempo. By noting
a small hand movement or a facial expression, one tries to
anticipate what the student is going to say or do. The discussion itself flips back and forth between competition and
teamplay. In short, teaching involves all of one's psychological
and physical being. Like a tennis player about to return a serve,
the teacher must be relaxed but alert, ready to respond to
whatever happens. The theory must be embodied, it must
become second nature, if one is going to be able to use it
unself-consciously.

How does one come to embody a theory? We may compare the process with the way we learn to speak a foreign
language. First, we isolate the skills or facts we need and break
them down into small units. (In language learning, we study,
say, verb conjugations.) Then we practice each skill until it
becomes unconscious and spontaneous. (We go to the language
lab to practice our drills.) Third, we use the skill in actual situations. (We try to speak spontaneously.) Fourth, we may review
our performance and work on any difficulties we might have
had. (We correct bad habits by again drilling those points.)

The art of questioning involves a similar cultivation of
skills. For a few classes, one may work on personalizing questions. One can develop one's technique, for instance, by imagin-
ing classroom situations and working out appropriate responses.
Then one can try the new skill in a real classroom discussion.
Finally, one should review the particular session (videotapes can
be invaluable) in order to see how one can improve that technique. When the skills become second nature, they become part

of the grammar and vocabulary of one's teaching. They become potential forms of expression, communication tools to be used as the situation dictates.

One final point about questioning. The more sensitively the teacher can use three-dimensional questioning, the more efficient he or she will become. If the discussion is too abstract, say, the teacher does not have to intervene by explaining, "We're getting too theoretical. Let us try to bring the discussion back to specifics." Instead, knowing from previous classroom performances that Joe is an especially pragmatic thinker, the teacher might simply ask, "Joe, can you see any practical applications for these theories?" In other words, the more successfully the teacher directs the discussion, the more it seems the discussion directs itself. The Chinese Taoist believes that the ideal ruler is invisible. The sage governs in such a way that the people think they do all the work for themselves.

Skillful discussion leaders use questioning in such a way that they seldom have to lecture; they become part of the medium of the discussion. The ideal is, perhaps, seldom realized, but it still serves as a goal for anyone involved in the art of questioning. The Taoist master, Lao Tzu, recognized the principle and the problem over two millennia ago:

> To teach without speaking, to benefit without doing—rarely is this achieved in our world.
>
> —*Tao Te Ching*, Chapter 43

CHAPTER FIVE

The Multifaceted Role of the Section Leader

Ullica Segerstråle

I
The Role of the Section Leader Within the Larger System

Writing a complete job description for section leaders is a formidable objective.[1] Even enumerating the explicit tasks of a section leader produces an impressive list. Practices vary from course to course, but on the average a section leader is supposed to do most or all of the following: be familiar with the rationale of the course and its requirements, attend lectures, prepare discussion sections dealing with the reading material, run the sections, give general guidance in the writing of papers and the execution of other projects, hold office hours, help students prepare for exams, and finally, grade the papers and exams. This is a broad and challenging array of tasks, requiring the development of many different skills.

But the best section leaders intuitively do even more. They undertake a responsibility which is rarely recognized: the major, complex responsibility of mediating between the students and the professor. Despite the time and effort this requires, they

---

ULLICA SEGERSTRÅLE, a member of the faculty at Smith College, received the Ph.D. in Sociology from Harvard, the M.S. in Organic Chemistry and the M.A. in Political Science from the University of Helsinki, and the M.A. in Communications from the University of Pennsylvania. She was a Fellow of the Salzburg Seminar (1974) and a Fulbright Scholar (1974). Her research and teaching interests are in social theory and sociology of science, with particular reference to the sociobiology controversy. While at Harvard, she taught sections in ten different courses.

1. I want to take this opportunity to express my gratitude to David Riesman, who gave me my first chance to test myself as a teacher of college students.

feel rewarded by the results: the professor feels closer to the students and enjoys the teaching more, the students learn more, and they themselves know that their sections are useful and integral to the course.

Learning how to play the mediator is not easy. It is often assumed that the only help the section leader needs to teach well is a number of tips on "making the section work," which mainly means getting a good discussion going and keeping it going. This training—particularly if it includes videotaping— may be useful, but by its nature it does not tackle the implicit out-of-class demands of the job. It assumes a smoothly functioning system without inherent problems.

This ideally functioning system can be roughly characterized by the following features: the professor has prepared an outline and a reading list and has clearly specified the course requirements. Students know whether sections are mandatory and how much section participation counts toward the grade. The professor's lectures are clear and interesting, making note-taking easy, and the students can perceive a bright central thread running through the entire course. The students find the reading list manageable, and the professor links the reading to the course in ways that help to structure the sections too. Exams are reasonable and the grading policy is fair. Students attend sections regularly because the professor has indicated at the first lecture that they are significant, either by making sections mandatory, by warning that certain important topics will be covered *only* in section, or in some other way. At the same time, close cooperation between the professor(s) and the section leader(s) is effected through weekly or biweekly meetings that focus on the reading materials, method of presenting the material, and *ad hoc* problems that arise in the course of the sections. At these meetings section leaders and professors compare approaches and evaluative criteria and decide how to achieve the desired level of uniformity among sections. The professors use this time also to ask for comments on their teaching, to find out whether the students are understanding the course. The atmosphere is cordial, the conversations productive for all.

Many faculty members (including the best teachers) are, in fact, very much concerned about teaching, and will take responsibility for these cooperative sessions. In one course in which I taught, for example, such meetings took place regularly over lunch, paid for by the professor himself; in another course the section leaders were invited to weekly dinners at the professor's home; in the third the professors and the section leaders were in close informal communication about a course that was well thought out to begin with, and in which the professors were regularly available to the students and the section leaders.

Often, however, the overall situation in a course is far from ideal—the system does not function smoothly. A "malfunction" in the system might involve one or more of the following problems, which directly or indirectly affect the section leader: 1) problems in the course as a whole and/or with the way the professor is running it, 2) problems in the relationship between the professor and the section leader, and 3) problems at the section level such as unsatisfactory student participation. This essay deals with problems of all three types, starting with those at the course level and moving on to a detailed discussion of section leading. As the reader no doubt already anticipates, the solutions in most cases often require a section leader to take more responsibility for a course than he or she, thinking about the thesis and the career beyond, intended or desired.[2]

II
Coping with a Conflict of Loyalties

The worst possible situation for section leaders could be some variation of the following grim scenario. The basic problem is that the professor does not have a clear preliminary idea of the course's content or aims. She or he cannot explain the overall rationale for including certain materials and excluding others, and cannot anticipate how far the course will go before the term ends. The professor has not decided on the requirements (e.g., whether there will be both a final exam and a final paper, or whether sections are mandatory)—or perhaps the professor has a clear idea of the entire course but in lecture is disorganized or obscure, in ways that make it hard for students to take notes. At the same time, the professor is

2. Most details in this essay concern sections in the humanities and social sciences, but some general observations and recommendations may be applicable to the sciences as well.

unaware of the students' difficulties and unwilling to ask for feedback. This professor has also little or nothing to do with the section leader(s).

One way to prevent some of these problems from arising is to make sure that the professor and the section leader(s) meet to discuss the course. If the professor does not initiate such a meeting, section leaders should make it their own responsibility to propose one before the semester begins. At that meeting they should ask specific questions about their role in the course: e.g., "What do you want the section to accomplish? How much leeway do I have? How much responsibility for grading? How can I get some help for my teaching?" This is also the time to make your own suggestions for the conduct of the course.

A preliminary meeting can be very useful. But even if the section leader adds many specific questions, one meeting cannot assure a trouble-free semester. It may take some time to discern the overall situation in a course, and problems may arise throughout a semester.

The conscientious section leader caught in a "grim scenario" clearly has many problems, but matters are likely to come to a head over exams and the criteria used for grading them. If the students have not been able to take good notes, should they really be given an objective quiz or an exam that is based on detailed knowledge that can only have come from the lectures? When the students do poorly, the professor may interpret the failures on the exam as meaning that the students are dull or lazy, not wishing to recognize that generally poor midterm grades reflect more on the professor than on the students. Aside from all the practical problems inherent in a situation of this kind, the conscientious young instructor confronts a division of loyalties: is a section leader's allegiance primarily to the professor, or to the students? This is a sketch of an extreme case. But if any of these elements exists, it presents a real challenge to a section leader.

There are two ways out of such predicaments. The first, which is swift and independent, has been wittily described by Jeffrey Zax in a talk for the Harvard-Danforth Center's Professional Training Series.[3] "The Teaching Fellow's strategy is

3. November 3, 1980. Available on videotape from the Harvard-Danforth Center's Video Laboratory. A version of this talk was published by the Harvard *Crimson,* on February 5, 1981, p. 3, under the title, "Feeling Caught in the Middle."

obvious," he says: "You organize a conspiracy." The gist of this method is to ignore the professor and do what you believe the students need. Zax gives several examples of the guerrilla section leader at work:

> Suppose the reading list in the undergraduate course is more demanding than in a graduate course. The professor thinks it's all very necessary and you know what he thinks. The students are never going to read more than a quarter of it and you know that too. Now you could keep quiet. Each student would guess at the twenty articles which will be most important, so that no two students will have read more than five articles in common. They'll all be petrified at the exam because they'll each be prepared to answer at best a third of each question and they'll do miserably. There will be no pattern to the ignorance and grading will be difficult. The professor will be horror-struck and his response will be to assign more readings. A situation like this can often be foreseen by the second week of the term.
>
> The teaching fellow's strategy is obvious. You organize a conspiracy. In sections you make it clear that a quarter of the readings are absolutely critical, double and triple asterisks, and you talk about which ones. At first this may feel subversive, but it's really a completely positive step. You are giving nothing away to the students, since whatever you say they are only going to read a quarter of the readings. You've certainly not undermined the professor, since now at least the class will be homogeneous in its ignorance. And the thing works itself out so much more nicely. When the test comes the whole class is well prepared for two out of five questions. The answers to the other three will be uniformly gibberish. So the two questions will be the basis of the grading, which is fair. Furthermore, any professor will immediately notice this collective myopia, will reconsider the readings the class seems to have ignored, and either cut them or improve them.
>
> There are many other opportunities to pull the same kind of maneuver. It's very popular, for instance, for a professor (especially in a survey course) to deal with an issue by taking two lectures and presenting all sides of the debate, all the strengths and weaknesses, and the names associated with each position. In order to impress students with the solemnity of the whole thing, he speaks of the interchanges with the kind of reverential awe that makes you feel the discussion has taken place at a very stately pace since the Middle Ages. And that's exactly what it sounds like to the students. The proof of this is that the instant they're asked a question, they ascribe opposing views to the same person, or they talk about the opinions and names they remember in such vague terms that they never positively associate one with the other. They hope you'll just impute the correct relationships and give them full credit. Here again, without hurting anyone you can make everyone happier by simply having an opinion. The professor will probably have summed up the discussion by indicating what he believes to be the truth of the matter, the academic truth, which amounts to saying that the question requires more study. That is not the same as the undergraduate truth. In sections you pick a likely

opinion and state that while it has not been conclusively
proven, for the purposes of the class it is correct. This may
seem overassertive, but it's not. It gives the students a chance
to bring focus into a subject that they would have ignored
altogether otherwise. And when the professor sees on all the
exams these cogent arguments all in favor of the same view-
point, he is going to rethink his own presentation. He'll be
surprised that his lectures were so conclusive, he didn't realize
he felt so strongly, but next year he'll be more explicit. Again
everyone profits.

The second strategy—mediation—requires tact and patience.
Its pedagogical first principle is still to put the students' learning before other considerations. But it aims, covertly, at getting
the professor to solve these problems or prevent them. In the
short run, it is a slower method, because it requires the cooperation of the professor. And it takes courage, since it requires the
section leader at times to take the initiative with a superior. But
its rewards are many—the section leader is not led to feel con-
spiratorial, and does not have to take on additional responsibilities that should belong to the head of the course. Of either
strategy, it may be said that "everyone profits." Temperament
may lead a particular section leader to try one or the other or
perhaps each in turn.

Whatever the problem may be, the first rule of the second
strategy is: do not treat this as an adversarial situation, but
rather as one of poor communication. The professor has to be
encouraged to become more explicit as quickly as possible; the
students have to be helped to comprehend the course, and they
have to be discreetly protected from possible disasters in the
exam. They do not need to know how nearly, but for the
intervention of the section leader, they would have been victims
of the head of the course.

In maintaining the delicate balance of loyalty to the professor and helpfulness to the students, the first thing for a section leader to do is to make sure that the students know the
course requirements. This may require reminding the professor
to announce them at the beginning of the course. On the first
day of section and occasionally thereafter, it is a good idea to
talk to the students about their degree of comprehension and
their note-taking. This can be done in an informal way. Students should not get the impression that they are obliged to
complain about the professor; there are, after all, many reasons
why individual students might have trouble taking notes. This
might be a good time to encourage them to ask the professor

questions in class or after the class hour (depending upon the procedure that has been adopted in that particular course). Another way they might improve their comprehension is by helping one another with notes and summaries of the lectures. Their cooperation will create a warmer atmosphere, and benefits may accrue—joint reports, more active discussion—that a section leader could not have reaped under an "ideal" professor.

If a pattern begins to emerge that suggests that the professor's delivery is the main problem, the section leader can still suggest various aids, based on general experience with note-taking and knowledge of the professor's intellectual style. Occasionally section time can be valuably spent explaining points that students did not understand in lectures and making sure that they now do. But the section leader is not a playback machine. If students continue to complain that they don't understand the lectures, the section leader can take down their complaints accurately and unostentatiously, and ask the professor for a meeting to discuss them.

That meeting will be more pleasant and more productive if it focuses, at least initially, on the students' difficulties, rather than the professor's communications skills. It is as helpful to assume that professors want to teach well as it is to assume that students want to learn. The key for the section leader is to outline the students' problems clearly. This will make it easier for the professor to anticipate the remedies. It is certainly better for the professor to suggest possible remedies than for the section leader to proffer unasked-for advice. If all goes well, the professor might offer to do one or more of the following:

1) institute a question period in class,
2) audiotape or videotape lectures so that students can review them,
3) write the topic of each lecture and an outline on the blackboard; spell all difficult names; write up dates; leave all material on the board until the end of the hour,
4) summarize a difficult argument at the end of the lecture,
5) hold a "question and answer" review session before the exam,
6) recommend secondary material or duplicate it and comment on it in lecture,
7) hold more office hours,

8) hold regular meetings with section leaders,
9) request an anonymous paragraph of feedback on the course from each student fairly early on.

In the situation where students have had problems understanding the lectures, and the section leader is afraid many students may flunk or do ignominiously on the exam, one approach might be to grade leniently without saying a word. The professor may insist, however, on a strict grading policy in connection with an unreasonable exam. It is better, in the interventionist style, to try to prevent this state of affairs from arising. What the section leader can do is to suggest to the professor a type of final exam that guarantees good grades for hardworking students even if they have not been able to take good notes. (This is also a good type of exam for those who have good notes.) This kind of final is based on essay questions taken from a master list of questions handed out in advance, about two weeks before the final exam. These questions should be creative and thought-provoking and they should require students to use the readings in the course as the basis for their arguments.

Students respond positively to this kind of exam. It encourages them to review much of the course material in a contextual way. Students who want to discuss questions together can do so; students who like to work hard can do so with the security that there will be no surprises in the final exam, and section leaders can use a rather strict grading policy without excessive anxiety about unfairness. If the course is a good one and the students would not resent a surprise, the professor might take most of the questions from the master list but have at least one unexpected question. Where this type of final exam is chosen the section leaders can be asked to contribute questions to the master list.

Regardless of the type of exam, grading the work done in the sections of a large course is likely to be difficult.[4] One of the main questions is whether the grading should be "blind" or whether the student's name can be known; another one, where there are many section leaders, is whether the exams should be graded by section or by question. This is another area where meetings uniting faculty and staff can be helpful. At first blush

---

4. For consideration of the general problems of grading, see Chapter Eight, "Grading and Evaluation," by Christopher Jedrey, pp. 103–115.

"blind" grading by question may seem fairest, but there are some drawbacks to it. First of all, a student may not regard each exam question as a totally separate entity and may not feel the need to repeat certain information in questions which are partially overlapping. If the questions are graded by separate section leaders, some points that sound vague but are meaningful in the overall context of the exam may be treated in an overly severe way. Moreover, if the section leader grades only one question he or she will not get enough feedback on how the students in the section are dealing with the course material in the exam. Feedback is important, both for the guidance of the students and for the improvement of the section leader's own performance. If the midterm exam is graded by section for these reasons, it might be fair to the students to use a pass/fail system, putting the grade in parentheses.

The interventionist approach may sound difficult. What section leaders need to remember while trying it is that we are ideally placed for mediating between students and faculty. We can identify with the professor, who is trying to bring order and clarity into a complex subject, and we can also identify with the student, who doesn't quite get the point. Developing this empathy is essential for any section leader, but we have to steer clear of the temptation to over-identify with one side or the other.

This means we have to overcome any desire we may have to awe and dominate the students. We have to suppress any wish we may have to conciliate the professor by concealing the truth about the faults of the course—or, alternatively, a desire to crush the professor by using the truth as a weapon. And these psychological demands may be complicated by practical considerations, if the professor also supervises the section leader's dissertation or is otherwise a power in the section leader's professional life.

The strategies outlined here do not guarantee complete success. Not every professor will become a hard-working ally. Some classroom problems a section leader must learn to handle quite alone. But these strategies can help us grow in the right direction. Both involve taking responsibility for what occurs in the classroom. By practicing tact with our professors, we learn to think of them as colleagues rather than superiors; by cooperating with them to produce the best possible course, we learn to think of them as partners rather than rivals. By behav-

ing always as if the students' interests came first, we come to
think of them as protégés rather than subordinates. We are,
finally, in the right frame of mind to face the micro-problems
of the classroom.

III
Making Sections Useful

The secret of section leading is not the thorough mastery
of the material by the section leader and the transfer of her or
his interpretations to the students, but the creation of a context
of *organized spontaneity*. The good section leader gives the
students opportunities and incentives to express themselves and
develop skills within the otherwise somewhat passive context
of a lecture course. All the pedagogical rationales for discussion
in small groups are related to these goals. The weekly section forces students to keep up with the readings and think
about their content, thus becoming actively involved in learning. Section participation trains students in basic social and
intellectual skills: understanding new concepts, listening to
others, learning to disagree politely, formulating an opinion
and defending it, criticizing the arguments of others, weighing
evidence. Sections use the excitement inherent in small-group
discussion to develop what may be lifelong habits of intellectual enthusiasm.

The critics of sections say that sections rarely succeed in
providing creative expression for all the students who participate; that they teach some students to improvise opinions on
call; that they make students needlessly competitive; that they
encourage some to substitute fast talk for thought, and drive
others to silence. These critics also point out that while some
students seem to enjoy sections, others perceive them as a waste
of precious time, or a humiliation. Indeed, even the defenders
of sections admit that sometimes discussions stagnate, that students do not always understand the assignments and occasionally do not even read them. They admit that it is easier for
instructors to fall into lecturing at such junctures, however
much they aim only to monitor free discussion. A dedicated
discussion leader, armed with practical advice, can, however,
prevent these critical situations from arising or correct them,

and can produce sections that will benefit all students to some degree.

Lively, intense discussions and true learning occur when the students' interests can be made to coincide with the material. Preparing this situation is so important that a section leader should "sacrifice" some part of the first section hour in order to bring out the students' interests and motives for taking the course, and should during the semester follow up strong personal feelings expressed by students about the course material.[5] In this connection, the section leader's own strong interests and feelings may prove relevant and even inspiring from time to time. On some occasions, as when a good general discussion of crucial issues in the course suddenly emerges, the section leader should be able to subordinate that day's reading assignment to the general issues, or may even decide to ignore the assignment entirely. Nurturing enthusiasm may require the section leader to give up a lesson plan on which much time was spent, or a list of quotations that would have built beautifully to some other point.

Advocating "free" discussion has by now become so standard that it is probably useful at the present time to argue for more structuring, if this can be discreetly imposed. The problem with free discussion is that it can easily become fixed on opinions, themes, or facts that the section leader feels are of peripheral value, at the expense of more central points. The section leader must make sure that the students follow the discussion intellectually, that they understand what is central and know when material is being misinterpreted by fellow students. He or she must be able to listen for valuable new ideas while stressing main points, providing logical coherence, and assuring the transmission of some basic body of concepts and general knowledge. If the section leader does all this tactfully, so that students are not discouraged from venturing their own interpretations and speculations, intervention should not be perceived as "undemocratic" or manipulative. Good section leaders learn how to guide without seeming to guide.

One way to have free discussions without chaos is to provide structure at strategic points in the semester through mini-

---

5. On the subject of getting to know your students, see also Chapter Two, "The First Day of Class," by Jeffrey Wolcowitz, pp. 10–24.

lectures or discussions on selected topics. Early on, for example, the section leader should make sure that students understand the underlying rationale of the course and know how the readings relate to the course as a whole. If the students do not see how readings and lectures go together they easily lose their sense of direction. By alerting the students to the links between the readings and the key concepts of the lectures, the section leader teaches the students to read in one of the "right" ways: that is, to look for the illustration of the concepts in the reading. At intervals during the semester, the section leader can also introduce "meta-discussion": fifteen minutes of brainstorming about questions to be discussed or concepts to be explained or themes that appear to be recurrent. The section leader can take these down on the blackboard and use them in planning future discussions. This type of brainstorming, where suggestions can flow freely, is a creative moment in the section. Searching for themes helps students to organize the course material in their own minds. Later on the section leader might ask students to invent questions for a hypothetical midterm or final examination. This exercise helps students to see the material from a teacher's perspective and gives them a better sense of the structure of the course.

Teaching students how to read a particular text can be one of the prime uses of the section. Students from different fields have a tendency to read material in different ways. In some cases, the main aim of a reading is to get an idea of an author's style and point of view, rather than to replicate detailed arguments or analyze particular passages. The more general approach, and the faster reading it requires, may not be obvious to students who are accustomed to reading their relevant literature word by word.

Primary readings can prove problematical in some courses and some disciplines where a text is used mainly to illustrate certain selected ideas, rather than for its own intrinsic value. Outside of a course on Wittgenstein, for example, few students can be expected to read his *Investigations* on their own, rapidly, and produce a comprehensive and well-balanced account of it. In some contexts, students may need to be given excerpts or clarifying secondary materials. Class notes may not always replace the latter, because a professor may believe that a particular concept is something that "everyone knows." The instructor can help by advising students to concentrate on crucial passages, and by going over the materials with them. If there is no suitable brief material available and students turn out to be puzzled about an important concept, the section leader should not hesitate to define and summarize and illustrate the concept.

Modifying sections in these ways may not please all students equally. Extremely knowledgeable or creative young people might have more opportunities to express themselves if the discussion were allowed to flow freely. They may also feel that increased stress on secondary sources takes away some of the excitement of discovering great philosophers and writers on their own, or deprives them of the chance of coming to an original interpretation of the material. These students may confidently be asked to read more fully in the primary material; so much the better for them if they are advanced enough to disagree with the secondary source! The section leader must be concerned with the average student as well as the very bright student who may have trouble with one particular idea or text; both run the risk of partially misunderstanding a great work. Some section leaders may also be uncomfortable at the idea of restricting their students' intellectual independence. I would argue that there are situations where it is better for students to get a mediated overview (however contestable) of a difficult writer rather than the diffuse and one-sided view which is likely to arise when they tackle the writer on their own.

The section leader is well placed to teach students not only reading skills but speaking and paper-writing skills and examsmanship.[6] One does so primarily by giving them practice in class in analyzing both lectures and readings thematically and logically, paying attention to the structure of arguments as well as their content. Teaching the forms of academically acceptable arguments is of course a task not only of the section leader but of every instructor in a college. But the discussion leader, unlike the lecturer, is going to confront at first hand students who do not know how to construct an argument. Typically they base a declaration on some long-held *a priori* moral, religious or psychological point of view. Some of these students are unaware of their assumptions; they have never been challenged, and they have no other confident mode of discourse. With vary-

6. On the topic of paper-writing, see Chapter Seven, "Teaching Essay-Writing in a Liberal Arts Curriculum," by Heather Dubrow, pp. 88–102.

ing degrees of rapidity, they can learn to argue on the basis of facts and logic; they learn to justify rather than assert; they learn to invent counter-arguments and respond to them. Before the section leader can deal with their assertions, he or she must recognize that these may be cherished and unquestioned beliefs, and that it may be very painful to unlearn them. Many crises and stalemates that occur in discussions can be prevented if the section leader is familiar with each student's level of discourse, and can therefore react to "primitive" modes of argumentation not with dismay or scorn but with sympathy and understanding.[7]

Practically speaking, the section leader has several chances to help students with exams. The moment when the first exam is handed back is a powerful time to reinforce what has been taught through lecture and section about the use of evidence, logic, etc. Students want to know why certain essay exam answers are right or wrong, and the section leader can review with them the main problems the students encountered, as a supplement to the written comments that appear on the individual exams. But it is important to prevent students from writing bad exams, by telling them beforehand about typical kinds of mistakes and by giving them suggestions about how to write an essay exam. The essay exam is a genre, and its typical properties can be taught like those of any other genre.

Two of those properties are comprehensiveness and specificity. Even good students sometimes "lock" themselves too quickly into one or two points in answering a question, expounding on these at length and ignoring other important points. I teach them to overcome this tendency by describing the process I imagine I myself go through. First, I resist the pressure to begin writing immediately, knowing I will do better if I think and plan my essay first. The question should inspire free association, bearing even on far-fetched and possibly irrelevant material. It results, predictably enough, in a sheet of disorganized notes, filled with pieces of knowledge, key words, names not to be forgotten in the rush to write down the answer. Reading the question again leads one to discard the unsuitable material; the ideas that remain are ordered to make the most persuasive case. Only then does one begin to write. The impor-

---

7. For a fascinating account of the epistemological process students go through, see William G. Perry, Jr., "Cognitive and Ethical Growth: The Making of Meaning," in *The Future American College*, edited by Arthur Chickering (San Francisco: Jossey-Bass, 1981), pp. 76–116.

tance of keeping an open mind, unconstrained by logical or stylistic considerations, especially at the beginning of a creative effort, is a secret not usually imparted by those who know to those who do not.

Providing the class with actual models of "good" answers to essay questions is a way to make them aware of their own thought processes and the properties of a good essay. Students who are puzzled about their grade have a model to compare their own essay against, and in class can derive a set of criteria to learn from. Often it is lack of models and ignorance about criteria of success that frustrate students and prevent them from performing well. If this approach is adopted, the section leader will need to point out that the model is of a possible approach rather than of an ideal content; discussion about the model will emphasize its rhetoric (its accumulation of evidence, its stylistic maneuvers, its persuasive structure)—those elements common to many forms of oral and written argumentation. The ability to present a convincing argument is certainly one of the major aims of academic training. The section leader can use the discussion format adroitly to try to eliminate, or at least diminish, gross discrepancies in reasoning ability between students. While all this is going on—and no one should expect rapid results—the section leader is also, of course, striving to control the other dynamic areas of discussion.

IV
Creating a Good Climate for Discussion

The atmosphere in the classroom emanates in part from the section leader's own temperament in response to the role: the climate is determined by the section leader's perceived humanity—intellectual openness, respect for others, gentleness toward ignorance, ability to convey warmth and enthusiasm for the material.

Instead of inspiring awe by trying to look like the professor—standing at a podium, dressing quite differently from the students—many section leaders find that they are more comfortable, and the discussions more relaxed, when they play down the "teacher role." One way to do this is to sit down in the midst of the students, thus communicating a willingness to be a participant in the discussion, rather than its master. In practice this means that the section leader has to arrive early enough to take a seat, arrange the chairs in a circle or a half-circle or around a table, and talk to students beforehand in an informal way. In conversation before class, the section leader can ask the students how they responded to the readings, and take cues from their answers to determine the course of the ensuing discussion. The transition between this informal talk and class discussion in earnest may thus be made pleasant and almost imperceptible.

Even the most relaxed and humane person may find that the class is silent, however, or that some students suffer from their own nervousness or others' malice, despite the good example before them. The practical suggestions that follow are aimed at increasing student participation and reducing tension—directly through stimulating and monitoring discussion and indirectly through eliminating potential sources of discomfort.

When young instructors find their generally bright and lively students taciturn, they sometimes assume that something is wrong with their own personalities or their discussion-leading skills. But this may be a false conclusion: in many cases students do not talk simply because they have not done the reading properly, and thus have no opinions. Section leaders can begin to correct this situation by asking students to refer to the texts in class, to make notes in the margins, and generally to use their books as references. Students without good memories can thus be encouraged to contribute, and all students eventually get the message that the text matters and requires close reading.

It is important to develop strategies that encourage students not only to do the readings, but to do them in such a way that they formulate opinions about them to bring to the section discussion. Short "opinion papers" have proven to be extremely fruitful in solving both problems. If a brief paper on some aspect of the current reading assignment is required from the students for every section meeting, this guarantees that each student will be a "specialist" on some topic, and will have a point of view already defended in writing. (In one class, these papers were up to five pages every two weeks, but the assignment could as easily entail shorter papers every week.) The section leader can use the writing as a basis for discussion by asking each of the students to present her or his chosen topic briefly—thus getting a general "map" of the interests of the class. In the process, the instructor can draw parallels from one paper to another, and ask some students to elaborate their opinions. Thus linked intellectually, students may begin to question one another and build upon one another's remarks. The section leader acts, in a way, like a successful host or hostess introducing people with common interests to one another.

Students keep these opinion papers during the class, to refer to them when they need to. The papers are collected at the end of the section and returned at the beginning of the next one, with oral and written comments. In one course in the history of science where this format worked very well, the comments encouraged the students to be more daring in their arguments and not merely reiterate the readings. This encouragement came as a surprise to many students, who enthusiastically responded in creative ways. One student, who wrote a hypothetical and very pointed dialogue between two scientists disagreeing about a crucial issue, was invited to read his paper to the section. We then offered the students the option of writing dialogues (substantiating their speakers' opinions with citations from the readings). Out of this freedom came some excellent, densely argued papers; fictional conversations, a couple of imaginary interviews, and even an annotated fable. A valuable extra from the instructor's point of view is that the weekly or biweekly papers make it possible to judge whether the students are learning to read and think in a more sophisticated way. In this course the quality of the papers steadily improved.

Writing papers regularly and reporting on them briefly gives the students training in structuring arguments for longer papers and exams, forces them to become well acquainted with at least some of the reading material during the semester (instead of saving the reading for a later cram at the end), and— by making them experts in some aspects of the material—leads to more intense discussions. Short, frequent papers can be a good substitute for either a midterm exam or a final paper.

Another effective way to build up to discussion, which also requires students to do the reading and become responsible for teaching one another, is to assign topics to volunteers and have them present reports during the next section meeting. These students can also prepare outlines for the class. In this way all the students in the section will be provided with some basic information to use in discussion, diminishing the discrepancy between the well-prepared and the not-so-well-prepared. Sometimes it is useful to assign two students to the same piece of reading and invite them to complement or question each other's presentations. The class discussion can easily take off from there.

Many problems in the classroom can be solved by using "difficult" students as resources, in the very situations in which one's first reaction might be to avoid or silence them. The knowledgeable and eloquent student, for example, who sometimes tries to dominate small-group discussion, can sometimes be soothed into self-restraint by being asked from time to time to expound on some area of interest. The ignorant but talkative student may become more cautious about jumping on the conversation, when given the same polite treatment. Instructors should never show by tone or gesture that they *anticipate* boredom or trouble from a particular student: this kind of type-casting handicaps the person's development, and insidiously lowers group morale. When other students give nonverbal signals that their long-winded peer bores or irritates them (tapping their fingers, doodling, whispering), the instructor need not leap to rudeness. A whole series of useful formulae— including "Excuse me, can you summarize your main point?"— are available.

In rare cases, a student directly challenges a section leader's authority. I know of only one such case, which occurred in a class where the section leader had been asked to lead a psychological experiment deliberately designed to frustrate the students. Sometimes the challenges are not so expectable, however, and they shake the frail self-confidence of the inexperienced. The best way to cope is probably to remain calm and friendly, and keep the issue impersonal. In the psychology section the student's anti-authoritarian behavior beautifully illustrated a certain psychological theory. There are few experiences that unify a section as much as a shared crisis, and few that enhance a section leader's reputation as much as maintaining intellectual objectivity in the face of a personal attack.

A section leader should be prepared to deal in the same diplomatic way with the student of special, unpredictable philosophical, religious, or political convictions. Such students may be voluble and dogmatic, especially if they are in the process of creating or losing their faith, or if they feel that their perspective is dismissed or ridiculed by their classmates. These students may become butts. They may arouse conflicts in the instructor's mind, compounded of distaste for the ideology and a strenuous ideal of fairness toward the individual. Unless the student's views are patently irrelevant, however, the section leader can use the occasion as an opportunity to "interview" the student, in a friendly way, about issues touched on in the reading. This will very likely clarify the issue as well as the student's position in relation to it. Usually the other students will take the cue from the section leader and will continue to treat this point of view as a resource. Thus potential embarrassment and anger can be turned into curiosity and inquiry, enriching class discussion.

Section leaders (like other faculty) need to be conscious that racist and sexist attitudes can and do erupt in the classroom. Without this consciousness, section leaders themselves may be guilty of discrimination. One form of it, hard to detect in oneself, involves treating "minority"[8] students differently, singling them out either by favoring them in discussion, or ignoring them. Videotaped evidence suggests that the minority student may hide at a corner in section, or give distinct nonverbal signals of discomfort/shyness/unwillingness to participate, which complicate the section leader's role. (Minority section leaders sometimes give some of the same signals.) While pejorative allusions to skin color seem to have declined, many women students complain that no such self-censorship inhibits pejorative allusions to femaleness. Women students have additional complaints about their educational experience: they say that instructors make eye contact more frequently with men, speak as if they were not present, interrupt them more often than male students, and deprecate women's studies.[9] They also sometimes note sexual tensions with male teachers or advisors, which make it difficult at times to have serious academic discussions. A lack of role models among senior faculty exacerbates all these problems.

In some areas of complaint section leaders are helpless: they cannot, for example, affect faculty recruitment of women

---

8. Women are often treated in the same way, and in the following paragraphs the word "minority" includes women.

9. These examples and others are described in "The Classroom Climate: A Chilly One for Women?" by Roberta Hall and Bernice Sandler (Association of American Colleges, February, 1982).

and non-whites. But the classroom is the focus of many complaints, and there the section leader has great power for good or ill. It goes without saying that section leaders should avoid racist or sexist language, and should avoid singling out particular students for special notice or neglect. In some courses, however, the situation of minorities may be a legitimate topic of discussion. Pointing out that authors on a reading list are members of minority groups is seen as a technique for reducing prejudice, as is suggesting additions to the reading list or recommending the works of scholars from these groups.

Discreetly helping the shy student is an inevitable part of a section leader's job—the student's minority status may or may not be an element in the shyness, and minority status becomes an element in the instructor's work here only if it prevents the instructor from noticing the problem or dealing with it effectively. Introducing students to one another at the first meeting, and getting them to work together on projects is pedagogically useful; that the camaraderie of a good discussion group reduces latent tensions is an additional benefit.

V
The Section Leader as a Catalyst for Learning

Some problems with sections lie beyond the individual section leader's power: the low esteem with which sections are sometimes regarded cannot be much affected by even the best-run section or group of sections, at least in the short term. My aim has been to suggest ways for a section leader to improve what can be improved within the existing framework: the relationship with the professor on the one hand, and with the students on the other. The students' needs must often be interpreted to the professor, the professor's ideas to the students. For the sections to be of optimal use to students, the section leader must (without neglecting other aspects of his or her career) assume a more active role than many section leaders now choose to take. In summary, this means working to give the section important functions within the context of the course, bridging the gap between the lectures and the sections as much as possible, and structuring the class discussion so that it permits a high level of student participation with no loss of content. Within the lecture-section system, the section leader is best positioned to teach major skills—reading, writing, oral presentation—and to guide the students' social and ethical development. Only the tutor and the professor who teaches entirely through discussion may have more influence in these areas.

The chief aim of a teacher, in the section as elsewhere, is still to make intellectual enthusiasm live. Without that, little real learning—and no permanent learning—can take place. There are no clear recipes for instilling enthusiasm: all methods are good except the bad ones, as one saying goes, and personality factors necessarily determine a section leader's style in approaching course material, discussion, and the students. Some will choose drama and conflict, others judicial equanimity; some will want to give mini-lectures, others will be self-effacing—and there are many gradations in between. There is one component of enthusiasm that all section leaders should be able to control, however, and that is the excitement of the "aha"-experience. By providing the students with the right tools and a congenial atmosphere, the section leader can increase the frequency of such moments of insight. And in that case the section leader might just have taught the students to learn.

CHAPTER SIX

The Rhythms of the Semester

Laura L. Nash

Of the many constraints upon teachers, the semester is probably the most inflexible; yet, curiously, this fact of pedagogical life is for the most part neglected in the large body of literature which exists on teaching. Far from being fully utilized, the semester is generally tolerated or ignored, with the same negligence that causes one to ignore the movement of the hands on a clock face. Through such indifference, teachers miss a great pedagogical opportunity, for the semester has a power and an organizational value which go well beyond its use as a bureaucratic tool (arbitrarily marking the beginning and end of instruction). If a course is remembered in and of itself, it is probably remembered as a semester-long endeavor. Will the semester be a series of separate sketches, as in a course in which ten different guest lecturers address ten disparate topics; or will it be like a framed canvas whose surface has been filled, inch by inch, with meaning and relevance to the whole? The richness of the final composition will depend largely on the professor's willingness to perceive the semester as a teaching unit and develop the course to exploit its unity.

Perceiving the semester as a teaching unit leads us to take a comprehensive view of what we want to accomplish. Once we

LAURA L. NASH is Assistant Professor of Business Administration at the Harvard Graduate School of Business Administration, where she teaches business policy in the M.B.A. program. In 1976 she received her doctorate in classical philology at Harvard University under a Danforth Fellowship. She has taught in Classics at Harvard, Brown, and Brandeis universities. Her current research is in the field of business ethics, on which she began writing and developing course material in 1980 as a Postdoctoral Research Fellow at Harvard Business School. Dr. Nash's publications include "Greek Origins of Generational Thought," which appeared in the fall 1978 issue of *Daedalus*, and "Ethics without the Sermon," *Harvard Business Review* (November–December 1981), reprinted in *Executive Success* (John Wiley, 1983).

understand the semester's potentialities—its potential rhythms—
we can make teaching decisions we may not have anticipated.
We can give students a coherent framework for intellectual exploration—which is what the word "course" originally implied.

Yeats's speculation, "How can we know the dancer from
the dance?" seems to me the most appropriate metaphor for
understanding the nature of the semester and one's role as a
teacher within this context, for although the points of access
to knowledge are multitudinous, in the traditional undergraduate experience the main entry point to formal learning is still
the university course, and the professor has the sole responsibility for the composition, choreography, staging, and performance of this very complex dance. With this metaphor as
guiding principle, Yeats's paradoxical question requires of the
teacher not just an ability to perform (a question sometimes
addressed by teaching manuals to the exclusion of all other
considerations), but rather the capacity to determine both performance *and* content, dancing and dance, and to hold them in
a balance which borders on artistry, as the title of Joseph
Axelrod's excellent book, *The University Teacher As Artist,*
would suggest.

The components of the semester can be likened to the
parts of the dance performance, with the melody equal to
the subject matter, the staging to the classroom, the mode
to the distinctive academic style of the professor, and the
dancers to those who participate in the class: students and
teacher. Timing, pace, theme, and variation—all the formal
components of a musical score and its performance—might well
be applied to the semester: just as the successful composition
rests first on an intelligible direction to the music and studied
variation within its movements, and then on the felicitous
performance by the dancers, so too the semester has its own
direction and rhythm which largely determine the final learning
of a subject. Thus the teacher is transformed from presenter of
wisdom to dancer and composer, responsible for the music and
for the way in which the dancers all work their art.

II
Preparation: Choice of Material and Mode of Learning

If the semester is a recognized fact of life, then the teacher's primary challenge is to maintain a controlled and compre-

hensive survey of a chosen topic over that period of time—
simultaneously to accept the constraints of the semester and yet
keep the students aware of the limitations of a semester's worth
of knowledge. One definition of maturity is the ability to
handle complexity, and in this context the mature teacher will
manage to convey a mass of material without implying that
students are leaving the course with a full mastery of the
subject.

As in a musical composition, an instructor should try for
variations of pace and mood throughout the semester, and most
important, a proportionality in the presentation of material,
a comprehensible arrangement of the notes. Unless the instructor must work from another professor's syllabus, choice of
primary reading will depend first of all on her or his own perception of what best represents the topic, a responsibility and
decision which are informed by past training and scholarship.
No generalized discussion of teaching can substitute for this
intellectual competence. Even when the content of the course
has been well represented in the choice of reading material, the
instructor will need more than his or her graduate education if
the material is to be presented most felicitously. This need for
teaching skill is equally great for teaching fellows, who may
have had their syllabi set by the professor: the fixed nature of
the material does not mean that its presentation is predeter-
mined. The content of one's classroom discussion is a personal
choice and responsibility.

At the beginning of the course, a teacher's careful explanation of how to use the semester's course material may directly
enhance or discourage student motivation and the value of
classroom work. The determining factors here are *access* and
pace, how and when a topic is introduced and how fast it is
explored. These decisions will depend very much on the nature
of the subject and the students' past learning. A semester progresses most effectively if one assesses *beforehand* the level of
learning required for entry into the course and then develops
course material which is responsive to and challenging on that
level. The kind of learning will also affect presentation of course
material. Will the pace vary depending on the difficulty of the
reading throughout the semester (as in an English literature
course), or will it steadily increase (as in a Latin translation
class)? Will the subject matter be closely interrelated and learning incremental (as in math), or will the topics range widely

and require the introduction of each as a discrete unit (as in the history of ideas)?

Each kind of learning has its own implications for student motivation and performance over the semester. For example, if most of the reading is included in one textbook, and classroom work consists of a set of lectures explicating that text, students may tend to allow the lectures to substitute for the text, and delay doing the reading until the end of the semester. A teacher's insistence on heavy and monotonous outside preparation for classwork, however, may cause students to stall out before the end. Both situations contribute to rising absenteeism as the course progresses. If the range of authors is quite wide and the reading list extraordinarily long, the chance increases that some of the material will be regarded as irrelevant and hence inconsequential. In each case corrective action should be anticipated and incorporated into the syllabus: a change in the quantity and kind of outside preparation at times not only avoids boredom, it also broadens the nature of the learning process.

Varying the reading material will correct such problems to a degree, but perhaps the most effective way to honey the medicine is by varying the classroom presentation. Standard techniques exist and are familiar to us all: the physics professor who illustrates Einstein's theory of relativity by personally imitating in exquisite detail a pendulum swinging in the universe (flail, flail, forward and back), or the English professor who offsets emotional discussion of "Prufrock" with a lecture on rhymed free verse. The guiding principles are relatively clear: *variation,* not just within a class but over the entire semester, in type of reading and classroom discussion, along with a deliberate *pacing* of the material which takes into account the nature of the desired learning process, together invite the students to steer a course in tandem with the professor rather than to lag behind out of boredom, overload, or confusion. Perhaps even more important, by surveying the entire semester's reading and discussion for content and by pacing the material, the professor illuminates her or his own understanding of the *purpose* of the course.

CLASSROOM HEART FAILURE #1:
THE MONOTONIC DISCUSSION FORMAT

Teachers frequently have a clear idea of where to begin a course, but a dimmer view of the semester's end. The conve-

nient constraints (chronology, the limits of a corpus, or the confines of a genre) only begin to narrow down the selection
process and will not answer in and of themselves questions of
larger purpose.

A thematic continuity, for example, without consideration
of the nature and pacing of the material will not insure a
cohesive and extended examination of the intended topic.
I once taught an undergraduate course at Brown on adolescent
heroism in Greek and Roman literature. While this thematic
focus provided the first determinant of the primary material,
the content of the course was equally shaped by several other
goals: I wanted the students to develop critical techniques both
in writing and in presenting an idea orally. I wanted them to
know the chief genres in ancient literature, to become acquainted in a general way with the major events of Greek
history and the Roman Republic, and to become aware of the
cultural associations which ancient literature made with adoles-
cence, and recognize to what extent these provide a basis for
our own concept of the phenomenon today. It would have been
very hard to rank each goal. It was crucial in such a course to
keep these directions in proportion, to find for each topic
a unique approach equal to the singularity of the content, and
to pace the course in such a way that the students would not be
required to learn how to write, read two epics, and review all
the previous reading in the last two weeks.

Self-discovery, rather than imposed analytical techniques,
was the desired mode of learning, and to this end I decided to
introduce each phase of the course through the students themselves, who were divided into small groups and given a set topic,
drawn from that week's literature, to discuss in class. During
the discussion that followed the oral reports, I would fill in
factual and literary information as it became relevant, question
their assumptions further when the class failed to do so, relate
the current discussion to past materials covered in class and
repeated in the literary tradition, and offer any aid I could
outside of class in the preparation of these presentations. The
students were highly motivated, bright, and energetic. By
setting these reports at the outset, we insured that we would
cover the assigned material.

Although I had considered content, mode of learning,
purpose, and pacing in preparing for this course, I still made a
terrible mistake. The class turned out to be much larger than

expected, but I was so devoted to the kind of learning experience which I described and had introduced before with some success that I stuck to this format. The pacing became deadly: too many people had to give a report each time, and we could not cut anyone off, because we had contracted for their presentations. Nor could we change the system in mid-semester. The only way to influence the pace of that course was in the management of the discussion: we held debates, we took on roles, we were asked to quote in detail, etc. Mostly we ran out of time to pursue their literary analyses in detail, and I tried to make up for this by offering rigorous questions and comments on their first set of papers and holding them to an expectation of significant improvement in the second set. The students were terrifically cooperative. Once they appeared in togas and wreaths, blankets and mud, and had virtually memorized the text of Aeschylus' *Eumenides* in order to debate the positions of Apollo and the Furies. Most reported that they learned a great deal in doing their own reports but became bored with listening to others'. For them the semester had largely become a single class (their own report), or at best two or three classes and a bunch of outside reading. Each individual class was significant to someone, and judged in those terms, the teaching was a success; but by the standards of a semester, it failed, and had I had a clearer goal of fully exploiting the semester, I never would have been so inflexible at the start. That painful experience impressed on me the need to consider the entire semester and the place of each class within that framework.

CLASSROOM HEART FAILURE #2:
TEN WEEKS ON THE FIRST BOOK
IN AN OVERSIZED READING LIST

In the above case the size of the class caused me to lose control over the classroom discussions, but a much more frequent error is to let the amount of the source material escape one's grasp, leaving five important books and three essential lectures out at the end of the semester. I call this the *gewissenschaftlich* seduction of the undergraduate teacher: ten weeks on the Pre-Socratics and one week on the *Apology* in a course on early Platonic thought; eight weeks on the Bolshevik Revolution with the one week of reading period to consider the rest of World War I. The motives may be intellectually pure—how

can you possibly understand Socrates' defense unless you have
some familiarity with Anaxagoras or Protagoras?—but the result
is pedagogically dishonest: the course will not be about Plato's
early period, and the student is left floundering with too much
important new material and no guidance just as the pressure of
exams begins. The usual justification for this is the warhorse,
"There's just not time in the semester; this topic is just too
big"; they imply, of course, that their knowledge is too great to
be encompassed within the given limits. This is not an adequate
(or accurate) justification; in fact, to use a phrase of V. S.
Naipaul, it is an applauded lie. Poor planning and failure to
control the classroom discussions are the usual causes. Students are the sufferers.

The semester is a neutral format within which one works
throughout one's academic career. Decisions about course
content should be partly institutional, taking into account the
major (will the Catullus course really contribute to the students'
ability to do Horace next year?), and the goals of a general
education ("That course really changed the way I think about
things!"). In the end it seems to me that these larger objectives
need to be examined explicitly by individuals and institutions:
by teaching fellows and their professors, by professors and their
departments, by departments and the faculty.

These questions should be asked before a course is offered
and the syllabi should be re-examined and evaluated afterwards,
so that true lack of accountability for content actually covered
may be corrected. This problem is particularly pervasive today
and is at the root of current complaints about the value of a
college education. It has given rise to frequent jokes among
students, who confide to their professors that they never really
learned to write in freshman English and never got to the
French Revolution in History 103, and so are in turn not
accountable for such knowledge.

III
Participants: Evolving Roles

Teachers. Just as the degree and style of learning during
the semester may vary over time and can be greatly affected by
the pacing and selection of course material, so too the roles of
teacher and student do not remain static. As Jeffrey Wolcowitz

points out in his essay,[1] the first class is particularly important in establishing these roles, consciously or subconsciously, felicitously or not, and greatly affects the outcome of subsequent classroom discussions. Again, a view to the whole will help anticipate and avoid some of the more common problems of student-teacher relationships, for if there is any certainty in teaching, it is that over the semester roles tend to *intensify.*

I remember from my own undergraduate days how much we tended to exaggerate and stylize a professor's manner of teaching as the semester progressed, and how much that communal image influenced the quality of learning. The contemplative—even eccentric—professor of physical anthropology, for example, took on the stature of Darwin to the students, who were inspired to pass the entire semester in methodic and directed examination of fossil remains. But the withdrawn passivity of the professor of religion, whose taciturn concentration on the text seemed at first romantic or just awkwardly shy, eventually became in our minds unsociability and intellectual arrogance. One slick lecturer, whose entertaining but endless utilization of anecdotes about undergraduate life excluded any serious consideration of Shiite Islam in a course on Middle Eastern politics, had by the end of the semester become nothing short of the Doonesbury Professor of Undergraduate Life Style. The teacher who recognizes this pitfall—that constancy of character may become caricature—runs another risk in trying to change. Any dramatic shift in tone made halfway through the semester may be viewed with alarm or mistrust. It would be foolish for a reserved person to strike a false air of bonhomie because he or she felt that a conversational classroom discussion was the only way to conduct a section successfully.

It should be possible to vary one's presentation as one's own pedagogical goals dictate; to hold the various roles in balance and let the teacher be seen alternately as scholar, world-citizen, mentor, private person. It is perfectly legitimate to teach Middle Eastern politics *and* offer lasting insight into undergraduate experience, if one establishes both objectives beforehand and weighs in advance their contributions to learning.

These considerations of public role are important and not just insignificant matters of style, because traits of character carried to an extreme can impede the learning process. For

---

1. Chapter Two, "The First Day of Class," pp. 10–24.

example, the teacher who remains the Super Student and presents the equivalent of a graduate seminar in each freshman lecture, may in fact confuse rather than enlighten.

While it is important to recognize and employ one's own personal style and taste, personal tendencies of character are merely one factor in determining a teaching style. Richard Sennett's idea of "public man" is strikingly relevant to teaching: it involves a *persona* clearly distinguished from the private self, formed in response to a common set of values and a socially determined idea of appropriate style. This persona is adopted because it allows social intercourse to occur more productively, and it works, as Sennett argues, ultimately to the fulfillment of the private self as well. When the intellectual journey is propelled exclusively by expressions of the inner self and personal scholarship, teaching can become rather narcissistic and limited. One example of this is the Super Aesthete, whose sensitivity to Blake is so profound that he or she regards it as being of first relevance in any classroom discussion of poetry—to the exclusion of such other nonessentials as literary tradition, genre and critical schools of thought. Any responsible preparation must conceive of the purpose for which a teaching style is adopted, a conversation in class begun, a lecture presented. The purpose extends beyond private motive to consider academic discipline, university culture and the nature of the student body.

Students. Of chief concern in the process of teaching is the potential growth of each student. A teacher's plans for the semester should carefully provide opportunities for students to change, discovering new and more mature academic selves. To what degree will the student operate as an individual scholar, wanting to increase knowledge for its personal rewards? Will the class seek wisdom collectively and judge success by communication within the group (as in a seminar), or will each student relate individually to the professor (as in a lecture)? Will the students and teacher progress in tandem, with the level of inquiry rising in unison, or will each student evolve as an intellectual soloist?

I think the general tendency is to adopt a mode of teaching and self-evaluation which comes automatically and then to work back casually to its implications for student learning.

These issues are examined, if at all, in retrospect. A class in which the professor lectures for the entire semester and evaluates student performance at the end through a paper and exam holds the student's academic role in suspense for rather a long period of time, and offers almost no acknowledgment of the student in the classroom. Hence if the student's learning evolves, only the student knows this. Learning becomes a product, a paper or examination, and as a producer she or he gets no chance for an external evaluation of that effort until faced with the ultimate and only test. This type of education relies heavily on the general cohesiveness of the undergraduate curriculum and places a heavy personal responsibility on both professor and student to conduct themselves effectively without overt feedback or external suggestions for change. At its best, this approach fosters each student's independent ability to study and evaluate material on his or her own, and is dignified by (or at least dependent on) mutual confidence and trust. At its worst, it uncovers problems only after it is too late to correct them.

At the other extreme, a class which relies exclusively on discussion groups assumes a complex mantle of relationships which neither teacher nor student is always prepared to handle. Failures and disappointments are monitored much more closely on both sides, and unless this monitoring is done productively, the participatory effort can work more harm than good. Here the perspective of the semester is an extremely important touchstone: there will quite naturally be variations of rhythm during these twelve weeks; one will see highs and lows of learning and teaching; discussion may be chaotic or interesting; repetitions will be boring impediments or useful pedagogical devices. The duration of the semester, however, allows time for failures to be corrected.

In a discussion class, individuality will be much more apparent; and if one sees the semester as a whole, these identities can be an invaluable aid to learning when the teacher takes the responsibility to turn them toward the subject at hand. For example, a young man whose parents were originally from Sparta and whom we will here call George once participated in one of my sections of John Finley's *Humanities* 3, which was a survey of Greek literature in translation. Most of our surviving Greek literature from the fifth century B.C. comes from Athens, and George's utter hatred of Athenian imperialism was strongly evident during the entire semester. Unconsciously we all began to play on the characterization of George as pro-Spartan and a critic of Athens; as it turned out, we used his role to identify the attributes of Athenian tragedy or Thucydides' history more accurately than we might otherwise have done. George and his growing number of allies intensified their role: we came to *expect* them to criticize Aristophanes' portrayals of farmers, and we were prepared to pull to the surface as countercriticism various underlying assumptions about the nature of the comic hero or the containment of Athenian farmers behind the city walls during the first part of the Peloponnesian War. In short, we had developed the discussion around identity; Spartan anti-Athenianism as personified by George helped us be more exacting observers of ancient Greek literature. Here again, one must use these identities carefully: if we hadn't turned anti-Athenianism to the details of the literature itself, George's charges would simply have become monotonous interruptions by the end of the semester.

Student-Faculty Relationships. I have so far kept student and teacher roles separate to the greatest possible degree while trying to suggest that the semester tends to intensify or even transform each, but the discussion-group class raises a third topic which must be considered further, and that is the inter-action of student and professor. Beginning teachers in particu-lar tend to feel the need to demonstrate to students their own *humanitas.* Closer in age and experience to the students than the full professor, anxious and concerned about their classroom success and highly dependent on student feedback, new teachers may set up themselves as model best friends, and like the friend in Plato's *Symposium,* who takes in hand the education of his beloved out of a "pregnancy of the soul" to beget prudence and virtue, attempt to engender and educe a learning process in others which is marked by virtue, beauty, but especially love.

It may be true that perfect wisdom can only be attained by a communion of friends, as Aristotle later argued, but the typical undergraduate class does not duplicate the conditions of the Academy, and a show of friendship must be carefully dis-tinguished from familiarity, which is much easier to achieve but often quite destructive. Students tend to be very generous with junior faculty people, and mutual identification can be as strong between students and young teachers as between puppies in a litter. Familiarity can increase at an alarming rate (again, one has the semester to intensify relationships), and when out of proportion it can lead to painful misunderstandings. The chummy teaching fellow or avuncular junior faculty member, whose first class is a resounding success at empathetic learning (in which trust and interest are immediately established by the teacher's approachability) may find that by the end of the semester the students are so totally familiar and friendly that they assume the teacher will automatically agree that they absolutely deserve an A, cannot finish a paper but cannot possibly qualify for an Incomplete, must phone at midnight the day after the paper is due to ask for an extension, etc., etc.

In a sense, this kind of familiarity and the desire to be "popular" with students can encourage a total abnegation of responsibility: for just as the student wants her or his work to be evaluated on the basis of friendship rather than academic criteria, so too the teacher may come to expect the same friendly standard of evaluation to apply to his or her teaching. Both parties can thus end the semester with a sense of betrayal, having lost sight of their academic purpose.

A second danger in the "best-friend" approach to teaching is the charge of favoritism. Like Caesar's wife, a teacher must avoid even the appearance of having favorites, flirtations, or special access (through common social or political interests, mutual friends, etc.). When a teacher fails to correct as soon as possible the impression left on the other students that comes from being accompanied by the same two students after every class, or from letting one overachiever take over the classroom discussion period, by the end of the semester she or he may have lost a great deal of potential participation from the other students. This is not to suggest that personal development, cultivation of character, and even friendship are not legitimate goals in teaching, but rather that one must distinguish between these qualities and the desire for popularity or parenting.

How then, aside from confining oneself to a formal lecture *ex cathedra,* does one maintain responsiveness and equal accessibility to all students? Again, time itself and the confines of the semester will aid in the process.

Junior faculty members and section leaders are frequently called upon to share personal perceptions of academia, women's rights, and Harvard's chances at the next Yale game, and in these functions a new teacher can play an essential role in university life. But nevertheless one's classroom identity needs careful and considered control. Certain relationships with students are totally inappropriate if not downright wrong. Neither the gossipy shared insights into Professor A's drinking habits nor a physically intimate relationship with a student have any place. A student crush, to which many teachers are tritely susceptible, may seem harmless and funny but should never be encouraged. More difficult is the sharing of a personal problem—a student in psychological distress may well want to talk about such a problem in the course of discussing his or her inability to handle the course assignments. Common humanity couples with academic concern, and one may find oneself deep into a student's personal affairs. In spite of an honest compassion, teachers can rarely help solve this sort of problem *while* a student is taking their course; and if it is of any magnitude, one would do best to guide the student to the appropriate counsellor with the proverbial gentle but firm hand. (Teachers new to an institution should familiarize themselves with its support services, for the sake of their own management of time, as well as for the sake of their troubled students.) One's own participation in a larger world—whether that of political activism, feminist discussions, or choral whistling—plays an important role in a university and can be a legitimate form of "teaching outside the classroom." But there is also an attendant danger: one may unconsciously allow students who share one's beliefs or interests special access during the semester, so that despite fair intentions, the teacher appears to favor them. Even friendships—and to me the extended sharing of students' academic progress and personal development is the highest reward of teaching—should be postponed until the course has ended.

If one seeks a certain well-defined level of communication with students, it is important not to rush the process, but to let the personal communication evolve naturally and inseparably from the mutual study of a given subject. Personal communication cannot be expected to be very well developed at the beginning of a semester, nor should one rely on this for the success of the first few classes. But if the classroom discussions, office hours, work on papers and reports are at all a mutual, cooperative endeavor, then the student-teacher relationships will naturally intensify with the semester's progression, and trust, individualism, and creative effort will naturally evolve.

IV
Special Classes

The First Class in the Context of the Semester. In Homeric times two well-bred heroes would never dream of getting down to business before the host had performed the ritual acts of hospitality: a basin of water if not a full bath, a comfortable seat, and food and drink were duly offered and accepted before either proposed to discuss an issue.

A first class has its own dynamics of hospitality, but unfortunately for the beginning teacher, they are not nearly as ritualized as they were in Homeric society. A generalized definition of these elements, however, will help the new discussion leader through this *rite de passage.* Again, the overriding context is the semester. This elusive phenomenon holds an essential place in first class preparation, for without a clear view of the whole to plot one's initial steps, the first class becomes such an overblown, terrifying, directionless onus that the sheer prospect of saying one's name and writing it on the blackboard before a group of strangers leaves one at a loss as to how to manage the rest of the hour. A friend of mine literally spent the two weeks prior to teaching his very first section walking around muttering, "Hi! My name is Tom White and I'm your section leader!" What most exercised my friend was the idea that the first class is an independent entity, an act of creation to be forever remembered in splendid isolation— especially by those students who choose never to return! To quote Robert Frost:

> You're searching, Joe,
> For things that don't exist; I mean beginnings.
> Ends and beginnings—there are no such things.
> There are only middles.

Rather than monumentalize the first class, one might better regard it simply as the semester's *point of access.*[2]

---

2. There are a number of ways in which an institution can cushion the shock for new teachers. For example, the Harvard-Danforth Center's annual Orientation and Welcome for instructors, which takes place on the Friday before classes begin, tries to alleviate first-day nerves. In 1980 and 1981, the panel discussions that closed the day's events concentrated on "The Worst Things that Can Happen in the Classroom and How To Deal with Them or Prevent Them," and "What I Wish I Had Known before the First Class Hour."

Drawing on personal preference, and bowing to the Homeric convention of giving each side a chance to size up the other gracefully through the mutual performance of clearly defined tasks, I tend to begin with the tangible, which is, of course, the syllabus—typed out, passed around, and introduced to let the students see the overall range of the semester's work. In discussing the syllabus, offering concern and direction about the availability of books, moving to the course requirements, setting office hours, one sets up the contract which Jeffrey Wolcowitz discusses in his essay, and gradually allows access to one's own critical predilections, rigor of evaluation, concern for the students' academic welfare, and interest in relating this course to their scholastic past and future.

When one finally proposes to discuss the subject matter, there remains that gargantuan unknown on which any participatory discussion hinges: the group itself. Since the character of the group cannot yet be judged, the chief questions are: how much class participation is desirable, and how can one achieve it? Are the goals to renew the students' ability to read Russian before tackling the first night's assignment, to acquaint them with the major Freudian schools before reading the great master, to display and reassure them of one's own competence in the field, perhaps to begin to get to know them personally (as in, "Now we'll go around the room, introduce ourselves, and discuss why we're here"), or simply to *engage* them in the topic? There are ways of doing several of these things simultaneously: presenting a strong quotation from an intellectual titan of the past, asking generalized questions about previous courses which they might have had in the same field (people who've worked together before will tend to find enough safety in numbers to encourage them to speak), or even taking a quick survey (voluntary and inviting only *brief* remarks) of people's perceptions of the topics: "What associations does patriotism carry today?" "What do you think of when we say 'China'?" "What makes a 'civilization'?" Listing the basic points of each answer on the blackboard will also direct attention to the subject rather than the person speaking (be prepared to suggest additional categories of thought when they run out). The best introductory questions have a direct purpose in the semester's life: as a reference point for the first two weeks of reading, as a melodic theme which will be repeated throughout the course, as a touchstone to return to, full circle, at the final class.

In the end, all that both sides can expect in the first class is a little better idea of what the participants are like and what the course is about. At the close of this class, after careful illustration of how the first discussion will fit into the rest of the semester's work, you may even discover that a definite excitement has been generated about getting into the course and working on the intellectual problems which you have proposed.

Intra-Semester Highlights. The semester has its own internal divisions which range from formal review points such as the midterm exam to informal cycles of rising and waning interest in the readings and discussion. At one time a course may occupy a very small space relative to a particular student's intellectual universe, and at others it may take on the proportions of a monstrous being. While there are no fixed semester biorhythms to which one can invariably refer, the concept of the rhythmic semester is useful for offsetting the general tendency to repeat a successful format again and again, as if the semester had no changing undercurrents at all as it progressed. Nothing is as self-defeating as the over-repetition of the same discussion structure. Say, for example, that one finds it useful to begin by reviewing the previous class and offering one last and challenging insight into that discussion. The value of this review may argue for its continued incorporation into each class, but there is no reason why the review always has to occur at the outset. One can refer back to the last class (or any previous discussion) as the point becomes pertinent—and if one has planned the semester so that classes have a perceived continuity, then there will be no lack of occasion for such a review.

As I've tried to suggest, the fully developed semester is no more a string of identical discussions than a great symphony is 400 repetitions of a C major chord. Rather, the semester needs punctuation points: new challenges to the critical competence which students are developing, reviews of work conducted so far, and explicit foreshadowing to stimulate their desire for future reading. In seeking variety, one can look to the material itself. Primary sources which require new critical tools or raise unfamiliar questions will create new forms of classroom approach as well. Even the university rhythm will influence the introduction of variations: the Monday after Thanksgiving, for example, might be a good time to suspend participatory discussion (and its extensive student preparation) and insert a desired lecture instead. The evolving roles of the participants might also dictate a change of format. In my Greek translation courses the students are asked, after they have gained a certain competence and familiarity with an author, to prepare an explication of a key word in the corpus, for which they must use a concordance, read extra material, and review the work read so far. They divide off into two groups, each taking a word of similar meaning (such as two different words for "wisdom"). In class each student presents one occurrence of the word, and the group discusses the variations of meaning within each word and vis-à-vis the other group's choice. The exam essay usually draws on this research and discussion so that each student has an opportunity to present as full a discussion of his or her own explication as possible. The development of philological tools, the growth of independent thinking, and their own discovery of the potential power of language, have been quite significant results every time.

Such an evaluation of the learning that occurs through this exercise is a dry, pragmatic assessment of something which is really quite magical, for if the choice of word is right, the session(s) can generate a natural summary of the whole course. I remember in particular a Homer class in which we examined two words for "fate": *atē* and *moira. Moira* (portion) turned out to have an almost endless variety of contexts, from a man's death, to a plot of land, to a share in a meal. As each example was added to the board, the class began to get more and more agitated—we were getting further from rather than closer to a definition of the word. The class abruptly stopped contributing examples—the perplexity had become too great. I knew in all honesty that no one word or sentence would adequately describe the meaning of *moira,* but I also knew that we had to make sense out of the chaos: we had horses, meals, dead bodies, booty, the gods, you-name-it, up on that board. In the midst of this silence I suddenly jumped to the board and very deliberately drew a circle around the entire thing. I asked one question: "Is there anything in Homer outside this circle?" We all began shouting and talking at once. It was all there: *moira* encompassed every aspect of Homer's world, and we had summed up the entire semester. The awakening awareness of the richness of a word like "fate"—no longer an empty term assigned to Victorian novels—was almost mystical among the group. It was intensified by their own diligent preparation (which had increased the perplexity) and by the group's having worked together through the highs and lows of translating the *Iliad* and the *Odyssey*. That punctuation point of the semester's continuity has been for me a constant beacon ever since in trying to hold a semester together while giving it pace and direction.

The Final Class. An economist was contracted by the *Times* of London to write a column which was to run 800 words. When asked how he managed to shape every topic to this length he said, "It's simple, when I get to 800 I stop."

Assuming that the ideal semester has a shape and direction, this artificial procedure is as disappointing as would be a sportscaster's failing to report the final score of the Superbowl because it was time for a commercial. Rather than flail through an enormous amount of new material, the final class should tally the score, review the semester's progress and the students' own development, perhaps return to the first class, and in short, hold the course up for examination and give it a finish. But the last class, like true scholarship, does not close the topic: the very final act is to break out of the frame, to direct attention to the next logical question, and most of all to leave the students not in panic but in perplexity. If the semester has been successful, it will have conveyed a mode of learning, and the students will be prepared to handle that perplexity productively.

My own final word on the semester is that one always has a *choice*. A teacher can ignore its constraints and possibilities, treating each class as if it had no relation to the whole, and leaving the semester as fragmented as shards of sculpture in a new excavation. Or the teacher can shape the semester into a well-articulated, organic form, reflecting the aims of the humanistic tradition in which we are lucky enough to work.

CHAPTER SEVEN

Teaching Essay-Writing in a Liberal Arts Curriculum

Heather Dubrow

Essay-writing resembles figure skating in a surprising number of ways, not the least of which is that the relevant skills are quickly lost if not practiced. A study has demonstrated that many undergraduates actually write better shortly after their freshman composition courses than when they graduate, apparently because they have not produced essays often enough or carefully enough in their subsequent classes. The abilities acquired in an expository writing program will be maintained and extended if—and only if—other courses regularly call them into play.

This is, however, only one of the many reasons instructors in all subjects, including those as far removed from composition as economics and engineering, should share with their colleagues in English an active commitment to helping students to write well. Instilling the ability to write clearly—and the desire to do so—is one of the central goals of a liberal arts education and, it can be argued, one of the responsibilities common to faculty members in a wide range of disciplines. Nor are the skills involved in composition unrelated to the ones taught in those economics and engineering courses: the ability to marshal evidence, the ability to organize ideas, and, above all, the ability to think logically are all developed by writing a paper. Moreover, in teaching our students about writing we are also teaching them about the subject matter their essays concern, whatever it may be: as instructors in writing courses so often remind their classes, style and content are really not divisible. Not only is an idea presented incoherently an idea lost to the reader; often

HEATHER DUBROW's biography is on p. 25.

that foggily expressed phrase mirrors a foggily conceived thought, and in the process of trying to write more coherently the student will be forced to think through his ideas more clearly. Producing a good essay can also serve to increase enthusiasm for the whole field in question, as well as self-confidence about one's own work in it, reactions that may well lead a student to learn more from reading and lectures and to participate more in discussions.

Motherhood has come in for attack from certain feminists, apple pie has earned the scorn of nutritionists, but clear prose remains an unassailed and unassailable virtue in the minds of most faculty members. Why, then, do some of the same teachers eschew all responsibility for their students' ability to write well, assigning few or no essays even in a course that would seem to invite considerable written work and devoting little attention to the papers that are assigned? Admittedly, time spent on improving students' writing is time taken from material more immediately relevant to the course. Tensions may also arise in our schedules, no matter how committed we may be to the importance of writing: marking essays carefully is, after all, extremely time-consuming. In addition, an inflated estimation of the students' abilities may make the teacher, especially the novice, hesitant to devote time to writing. (In particular, major universities too often foster a conspiracy of silence: the faculty assumes that someone else must surely have taught these highly select undergraduates the principles of, say, punctuation or prosody or primogeniture, while students respond to the assumption that they already know elementary material by becoming increasingly ashamed to admit that they do not know it and hence increasingly unlikely to remedy the deficiency.) Another reason we may be reluctant to help our students with their writing is that composition programs are so often the stepchildren of university faculties. Unfortunately, certain professors believe that those who can, teach, while those who cannot, teach writing; conscious of this attitude, teachers may hesitate to express a serious interest in composition. Perhaps the most subtle conflict that arises when we try to improve students' writing, however, stems from the fact that few of us write with complete confidence and ease ourselves. Here, as in so many other areas of teaching, the willingness to admit our limitations is more than half the battle: a student will learn far more, both by precept and by example, from the teacher who, acknowledging that he or she is not sure of a grammatical rule or stylistic principle, offers to check on it, than from the one who nervously skirts the relevant principle when grading or discussing a paper.

Because essays serve so many different functions, they may be integrated into our courses in a number of different ways. Should one assign one long paper or a few shorter ones? At what point in the term should the written assignments be due? Behind these issues lies a larger pedagogical question: to what extent do we regard papers as a tool for educating our students, to what extent as a means of evaluating them? The former assumption may lead us to require that the class submit several papers, with at least one due early in the term, so that they may take our reactions to their initial written work into account when preparing subsequent papers. Many teachers choose to assign at least one essay within the first month of the semester. This encourages students to become engaged with the course, while at the same time helping the instructor to identify anyone who is having trouble with the material before the semester is too far advanced. If, however, essays are to weigh heavily in grading, some teachers argue that one should require only one paper, due at the end of the term, since at that point it can fairly be used to judge the writer's grasp of the whole course. Fortunately, these approaches are not mutually exclusive: in most discussion or lecture courses one could assign both a brief essay early in the semester and a longer one later on, while tutorials permit and encourage a whole series of written exercises.

Other complicated decisions include the type of topic to assign and whether, indeed, one should offer assigned topics at all. Some courses virtually demand research papers, others virtually preclude such assignments, while in yet others the teacher faces considerable latitude. Here, too, compromise can be useful: another reason for asking students to write more than one paper is that they can then get experience with different types of exercises. Certain teachers swear by assigned topics on the grounds that this policy ensures that their students write on a subject that is both significant and manageable, while others assert that choosing their own topics teaches students how to define and delimit their material as well as making them more enthusiastic about the paper. Another possibility is providing a list of suggested topics but appending to it the information that the student may instead devise his own— as long as she or he clears it with the instructor before writing. When that proviso is included, it needs to be presented firmly and clearly, possibly even with serious sanctions (e.g., "I will not accept an essay if its author has not previously cleared the subject with me"): too many students check with the teacher only when the paper is close to completion.

But the most skillfully crafted topic is wasted if the student is unable to work on it effectively. One of the first steps in helping our classes with writing is anticipating the problems, psychological and practical, that they are likely to encounter. Not the least of those problems is the tendency to put off writing the essay. As Dr. Johnson reminds us in a *Rambler* essay on procrastination, "even they who most steadily withstand it, find it, if not the most violent, the most pertinacious of their passions." This pertinacious passion is often exacerbated by a myth that is very common among undergraduates, the notion that the really bright student effortlessly tosses off his or her papers at the last minute. According to this myth, a latter-day version of the Renaissance ideal of *sprezzatura,* or cultivated ease, the elect need not work hard on essays, or anything else, to produce impressive results. Their papers flow smoothly from their typewriters in a mere hour the night (or the morning) before the deadline, an hour perhaps sandwiched between reporting on the asbestos in the college tunnels or the roaches in the college food for the student newspaper and performing with effortless ease on the viola da gamba. Admitting to oneself or to others that one is laboring over an essay can appear to be an admission that one does not rank with the elect, with those truly brilliant students who need not work hard.

Students also may delay writing simply because they have several assignments due at once and are inexperienced in planning their time. In other instances the writers start an essay at the last minute to provide themselves with an excuse if it does not turn out well: they persuade themselves that, had they had the requisite time, they could have avoided the flaws that, as they uneasily suspect, are really inherent in their writing. Difficulty with essays may, of course, signal other and deeper problems, such as an obsessive desire for perfection (such students often retype each page of a rough draft if they make even a small mistake) or an unwillingness to trust one's own judgment about the most minor details of writing.

All of these issues remind us again that informal counseling is inextricably connected to teaching. One of the principal ways of helping the class as a whole to write well is to warn the group about the importance of starting papers early and the temptations not to do so; and one of the principal ways of helping individual students is to be alert to the fact that for any one of a number of reasons they may be finding it very hard to get to work on the paper.

Certain of the difficulties that I have been enumerating may, of course, require professional help. You should familiarize yourself with the services your institution offers, and recommend them as early in the semester as you can. You are not insulting students by making such recommendations: on the contrary, you may not only be easing your own relationship with them at the time, but also helping them solve a problem once and for all.

Justice Brandeis once observed that there is no good writing, only good rewriting. This may well be the single most important truth about expository writing that we can offer our students. That myth of the brilliant last-minute job mitigates against careful and thorough revision, as does a basic misunderstanding of the very process in question: even students who are strongly committed to producing good essays often assume that editing involves little more than glancing over the rough draft before retyping it, perhaps adding a sprinkling of commas as one goes through. One of the most fundamental ways of helping students to write well, therefore, is simply explaining why revision is an elaborate and time-consuming, though rewarding, activity.

The next step is anticipating and attempting to alleviate the more technical difficulties that students face. Strikingly similar problems confront undergraduates even when they compose papers in strikingly different disciplines. Whatever the subject of the course, many members of the class will benefit from advice about how to argue their points effectively. Like writers at all levels, undergraduates are often so involved in their subject that they fail to explain their ideas fully enough or to substantiate controversial theories; they need to be reminded that the insights that they themselves have lived with for weeks may be far less familiar to the reader. When assigning research papers, it is useful to stress that such essays do not preclude and, indeed, often invite original thought: without this warning, many students are prone to produce a mere compilation of other people's ideas on the topic, rather than evaluating and extending those ideas.

Diction can also prove problematical. In essence, students need to learn the traditional concept of decorum: particular styles are appropriate to particular modes of discourse, and consistency within the chosen style is usually a virtue. The idea that an essay should be more serious in tone than everyday conversation, however, often generates the misconception that it should be needlessly and awkwardly formal. When they are not confident of their ideas, undergraduates (not unlike their elders and betters in and out of the university community) tend to embellish their prose with long words and elaborate constructions. Often, too, a student will stud his paper with far too many technical terms simply because he or she is pleased to have mastered some of the terminology of the field and eager to demonstrate that mastery. The distinction between adducing the necessary technical vocabulary and indulging in unnecessary jargon is a fine but important point; one basic rule of thumb is that technical terms should be avoided unless they express the point more clearly or more economically than could otherwise be done.

Many essays are flawed by another kind of jargon—that offered by popular culture. Students are seduced and betrayed by the media, as well as by political speeches, into coining adverbs by pasting "-wise" onto words and into repeating catch-phrases like "at this point in time." Other problems in diction may be traced to the belief that one can polish one's writing (or simply impress one's teacher) by frequently consulting a thesaurus. Undergraduates often need to be warned of the dangers of substituting a "synonym" whose connotations may in fact differ significantly from those of the word they had originally intended to use.

Even more fundamental and more technical problems frequently confront students. A number have never learned the basic rules of punctuation; many have trouble with paragraphing. Seemingly local problems like these may in fact generate other and deeper ones. Because they nervously realize that they know nothing about, say, the care and feeding of the comma, students may lose confidence in their ability to write and hence approach essay assignments with considerable trepidation. And in writing, again as in figure skating, a loss of confidence can quickly lead to a loss of skill.

Given that difficulties like the ones I have been enumerating are as profound as they are pervasive, how can one incorporate some attention to them into a course without siphoning an inordinate amount of time away from classes on the crisis of the aristocracy or the structure of the cell? Many instructors append some guidelines to essay topics ("If you choose this subject, be especially careful not to waste too much space on plot summary") or preface the entire list of topics with general suggestions ("Much of the research in this area is controversial, so be sure to consider the underlying biases of the studies you cite"). Certain teachers instead—or in addition—supply a separate sheet with instructions about composing good essays. Such a form can be designed so that it applies to all of one's courses, with information specific to only one class perhaps added orally during a class meeting or provided on the assignment sheet. These instructions may include general rules about composing good papers ("Be sure to include enough quotations to back up your assertions"), reminders of grammatical and stylistic principles ("Adopt a consistent policy about how you refer to yourself"), and practical advice ("Leave margins of at least 1½ inches all around the paper to allow space for my comments").

One can also help students by recommending some of the inexpensive and readily available books that offer guidelines about expository writing and themselves exemplify clear prose. Many instructors swear by William Strunk and E. B. White, *The Elements of Style*, a concise and witty commentary. George Orwell's "Politics and the English Language" (included in Orwell's *A Collection of Essays*) argues that political confusion is reflected in and generated by linguistic confusion; this essay would thus be an obvious choice in government or history classes. It has much to offer students in other disciplines, however, notably a list of sane and simple rules about writing: "Never use a long word where a short one will do. . . . If it is possible to cut a word out, always cut it out. . . . Break any of these rules sooner than say anything outright barbarous." *The Lives of a Cell* and *The Medusa and the Snail*, compilations of Lewis Thomas's columns on science, include several cogent essays on expository writing. One of the most delightful,

"Notes on Punctuation," includes (unlikely though it may seem) a panegyric on the semicolon.

It is often useful to provide students with models by passing out and perhaps briefly discussing a successful essay, as well as excerpts from unsuccessful ones. Moreover, the students whose papers are chosen as instances of good writing may well be pleased and heartened by the compliment. But proffering samples of good and bad prose can prove problematical. Even if one adopts the expedients of presenting the examples of weak writing anonymously and requesting permission from those whose papers will be discussed, members of the class may come to feel jealous if one student's papers are repeatedly held up for admiration or hurt if their own are repeatedly attacked. One solution is to cull one's samples of both good and bad writing from many different essays; another is to use papers handed in during a previous term.

When one's own schedule permits, one of the best ways to help students to revise carefully is to collect and comment on their rough drafts, perhaps even indicating that the final product will be judged not only in terms of its intrinsic merits but also in light of the extent to which the rough draft has been improved. If I have not been able to examine a preliminary draft before the essay is due, I have often asked students to submit the rough version together with the final one. I stress that I am doing so not in order to evaluate the preliminary work per se but rather to judge the extent to which it has been successfully revised. This policy encourages the students to rework their rough drafts more thoroughly than they might otherwise have done (it also makes plagiarism more difficult).

Students are often intrigued when they compare the rough drafts produced by more experienced writers with the final version: by bringing in a few pages from an early and a final draft of one of their own essays and explaining the changes, instructors can effectively demonstrate the process of revision. Another reason it is useful to display one's early drafts is that students often assume that they are alone in finding essay writing difficult and painful. The fact that a more senior person in the field also must, as it were, expend blood and sweat and tears on the process may prove disheartening to a few students, but most find it reassuring.

Valuable though lists of guidelines and models of essays may be, there is no substitute for devoting at least ten or fifteen minutes during class to talking about an essay assignment. One can cover a surprising number of points in that time. What we are doing during those minutes, however, is quite as effective as whatever we may be saying; the very fact that the instructor takes expository writing seriously enough to devote some class time to it invites the students to take it seriously. One can underscore the importance of this discussion by listing it on the syllabus—a policy whose added advantage is that students are likely to attend classes advertised as providing advice on essays, fearing that otherwise they may miss information essential to performing well.

Teachers sometimes fear that they will insult or frustrate their classes by devoting even a few minutes of a course on a subject like the organization of Mayan culture to the organization of essays. While a few undergraduates may resent such a discussion, a surprising number are very much aware of the deficiencies in their own papers and eager to remedy those problems. Many of the attitudes that we decry in other circumstances work to our advantage here. However pernicious the growing emphasis on pre-professional and vocational education may be, it has at least bred the awareness that many graduate schools and many employers do check to see if their candidates can produce good prose. However damaging anxiety about grades may be, it at least carries with it the likelihood that the student will listen with eagerness, not hostility, if the teacher devotes some time to talking about writing.

Private conferences, devoted either to discussing an essay prospectively or to analyzing it retrospectively, are another good way of improving writing. While part of a one-to-one tutorial meeting can be allotted to talking about writing, offering conferences in a larger course proves very time-consuming. But it is time well spent. Students often learn more from a personal discussion of an essay, however brief, than from written comments. Without conferences some undergraduates, unfortunately, would tend to focus on the grade and only glance through the instructor's annotations (even if these have been meticulously crafted in accordance with the principles in this chapter). And the many students who do read written comments with care are grateful for the opportunity to discuss and perhaps disagree with some of the teacher's evaluations. Other benefits of those conferences are more subterranean but often no less significant. The very act of offering conferences on essays, like that of spending class time discussing them, demonstrates one's commitment to writing. And students who speak with an instructor during her or his office hours—however briefly and on whatever subject—often prove more willing to participate in class subsequently.

One problem that confronts and often confounds the novice teacher is a request for an extension. Many instructors honor such requests routinely, recognizing that other course work may make it difficult for even the most conscientious student to complete a given assignment on time (and perhaps also remembering how often they themselves were grateful for extensions). Others, however, extend essay deadlines reluctantly if at all. Doing so, they maintain, is unfair to the people who have handed in their work on time and may also merely provide a license for procrastination. One compromise is to give extensions if the reasons seem valid but to insist that they be arranged before the paper is due and to specify a new due date; these policies help the student to feel more responsible about deadlines and also ensure that the instructor is not inconvenienced by waiting for a paper that mysteriously fails to appear. The whole problem of extensions can, however, sometimes be skirted if one's deadlines come relatively early in the term and hence do not conflict with other assignments.

Like other literary genres, essay comments can and should reflect the style of the individual teacher—some, for example, prefer extensive margin comments and a brief summary at the end, while others reverse the balance—but a few general principles do apply across the board. Students become upset, and rightly so, if their instructor takes an inordinately long time to return their essays. If one is assigning papers oneself rather than assisting in a course whose deadlines are set by another instructor, one can often avoid this problem simply by staggering the due dates in one's different classes, thus ensuring that one is not confronted with papers from the forty-one students in one course, a set of quizzes from those in another course, and an impending deadline on one's research all on the same Friday afternoon.

While determining an acceptable interval between the collection and the return of essays is difficult, depending as it does on the nature of the course, the number of other assignments, and so on, in general if more than three weeks have passed before the paper is marked, students are likely to have lost a lot of their interest in it and perhaps a lot of their respect for the teacher, responses that may well affect subsequent performance in the course. But on this, as on so many other issues in teaching, frankness can be very helpful. The same students who would become quite hostile if a set of papers were held for a month without any excuse are likely to accept the situation if the teacher explains that a thesis deadline impends or that he or she is busy marking papers from another course.

Few things are more discouraging to a student than to receive a brief and hasty comment on a paper to which she or he has devoted considerable attention, even if the comment is favorable. On the other hand, well-meaning teachers sometimes run the risk of discouraging the author by offering too many suggestions. One simple way of making annotations seem less overwhelming is to avoid red ink, which can connote harsh judgments despite the fact that the actual comments in question may be mild or even favorable. (I myself learned this the hard way when a student responded to a paper that I had conscientiously deluged with comments in red ink with a telling comment of his own: "It looks like you bled all over the essay.") In any event, we should remember that because some instructors comment at length only on a disastrous paper, many students panic, at least momentarily, if an essay is returned with copious annotations. It can be useful to warn them beforehand that such annotations signify not that they have done a bad job but rather that you are trying to do a good job.

Students appreciate praise that is specific enough to show them what strengths they should maintain and develop: "A good job in many ways" is far less useful than "You evaluate the historiographical problems judiciously and succinctly." It is tactful to precede one's criticism with at least a brief allusion to the virtues of the essay, even if there are not many. And, of course, even if one is marking an unconscionably bad paper at an inordinately late hour with an indescribably bad head cold one should be measured in those criticisms, avoiding the temptation to bolster one's own ego by inflicting snide comments on the author. We also need to beware of another source of snide comments, our irrational resentment at student errors; it is as hard as it is necessary to remember that such errors generally do not reflect malice or hostility towards us.

In addition to being measured, criticism, like praise, should be specific. A vague judgment like "major methodological problems" will not help the writer to avoid those problems in the future. One formula that sounds appropriately constructive (and also avoids the danger of discouraging the student by implying that virtually everything about his essay needs improvement) is: "In your next essay, concentrate especially on improving 1) . . . 2) . . . and 3). . . ."

Many teachers keep a brief record of the strengths and failures of each student's papers so that they can refer to earlier work when commenting on the essay in hand—"I'm pleased to see that you are avoiding the vague generalizations that weakened your first paper." Such annotations also prove useful when one is asked for recommendations.

Commenting on stylistic and grammatical problems poses special difficulties: one needs to convey one's criticism briefly, and yet if one merely writes, say, "diction" in the margin, one risks confusing the student who is not familiar with the term, let alone with the way it may apply to his paper. We can adopt the expedient of referring students to grammar books, but only if we know that they own such texts. I myself have been experimenting with one way of commenting concisely but clearly on problems of style, grammar, and presentation: I have prepared and duplicated a series of about twenty slips of paper, each of which covers a particular flaw, defining technical terms when necessary and suggesting ways of avoiding the error. My sheet on dangling modifiers, for instance, explains what that problem is, cites examples of it, and shows how the sentences in question could be corrected. When a student makes a technical mistake, I simply attach the relevant slip to his essay, if necessary putting an asterisk on the section of the slip most closely connected to his own mistake. It is likely that members of the class read these sheets with more care than they would an allusion to a grammatical or stylistic concept that they may not fully understand, and the sheets spare me the frustration of trying to cram the same information about dangling modifiers into the margins of half a dozen different papers.

Assigning grades to essays often proves far more tricky than writing comments on them; teachers who would unite in condemning a comment like "This paper is a disaster from start to finish" often would disagree, and disagree intensely, on how to grade that or any other essay. Many students expect that the amount of work they put into an essay will be considered in the final grade; some instructors emphatically endorse this assumption, while others just as emphatically reject it. Another issue is whether one should consider improvement in grading essays. In so doing we may in effect penalize the student who has done superior work from the beginning of the term; on the other hand, it may seem only fair to reward improvement, and doing so certainly provides an incentive for hard work. In any event, in practice acknowledging improvement by raising the grade can become complicated, especially in a course involving many essays, such as a tutorial: when we raise each successive mark to indicate that the author is successfully avoiding some of the faults that marred his earlier work, we soon find ourselves assigning a grade noticeably higher than the paper might merit if merely weighed in isolation. One can sidestep this difficulty by starting out with very low grades, but that policy should in turn be adopted only with caution: receiving an extremely low mark, especially if they suspect that it is not deserved, may discourage students so much that they despair of ever doing better and devote too little effort to subsequent work in the course. Whatever decisions we may reach about these problems in grading, here, as in so many other situations in teaching, one should spell out one's policy clearly and apply it consistently.

Another type of decision will be reflected in our answer to the question, "Mr. Jones, do you mark for style?" This query often carries with it a hostile undercurrent: "Mr. Jones, surely you don't mark for style in a government course. If you were an English teacher I could understand your caring about that sort of thing, but as it is. . . ." Obviously, each instructor must decide the extent to which he or she will consider style in grading. But, even leaving aside the point that unsuccessful writing is often related to vague thinking, Realpolitik suggests that we show our concern for writing, and encourage a similar concern in our classes, by considering it to at least some extent when determining grades.

One of the most effective ways of encouraging good writing is to encourage good rewriting by building into the course some opportunities for revising papers that have been previously submitted. Tutorial is an excellent forum for this sort of work; some tutors regularly ask their student to rewrite some or even all of their tutorial essays. We can also offer students the option of reworking a less than successful paper; one can make this suggestion more attractive by weighing the second grade more heavily, or even by counting it alone. When one does offer such an opportunity, though, it seems fairer to give it to the whole class. If an essay is so disastrous that one could in all conscience assign only a very low grade to it, often the student will learn more (and feel less discouraged) if her or his work is returned ungraded but with judicious suggestions and the request that it be revised. Since many undergraduates, unfamiliar with the complexities of revision, assume that they should merely change the paper in accordance with the teacher's comments, it is often useful to point out that one expects a more thorough and more thoughtful reworking than that if a paper is to be rewritten.

Though this chapter has been prone to rank the process of assigning essays very close to godliness and way ahead of cleanliness, papers are not, of course, the only kind of exercise we may employ or even, under some circumstances, the best one. While oral reports cannot teach students certain important writing skills, notably those involved in polishing one's style, they do provide training in other and equally important skills, such as organizing ideas and presenting them clearly. Delivering reports can obviously help undergraduates to learn to speak effectively, and responding to queries during the question period can build some of the same abilities that a discussion course as a whole develops, such as thinking clearly and arguing coherently. Reports also offer an indirect but not unimportant benefit: when they are well presented and openly appreciated by the teacher, members of the class will realize that the people delivering them are raising interesting and important points. This recognition helps the class to abandon an assumption that is singularly destructive to learning in general and learning within a small group in particular—the assumption that comments by other students deserve infinitely less attention and respect than those offered by the instructor.

But, like so many other blessings in life, oral reports are at best a mixed one. Because they make life easy for the teacher by filling class time, a little soul-searching is called for before we build them into a course: we should carefully review their inherent disadvantages to be sure that reports are on balance worth including. Often the audience becomes bored and learns little (a generalization many teachers could second from their own memories of certain graduate seminars). As was noted in the chapter on lecturing, attention spans are usually quite limited, and this problem is exacerbated when the student delivering the report has not had enough experience in public speaking to know how to hold the audience's interest. One solution is to assign only very short presentations (say, around ten minutes) and firmly enforce that time limit, which is often a difficult task. Also, though reports are often used to introduce material that the rest of the class has not read, students in fact generally listen much more closely to reports if they already have some familiarity with what is being discussed.

Shorter written exercises can also be useful supplements to papers. A number of teachers, expecially those in literature courses, ask their students to keep journals, making an entry on each book they read. Journal entries do not offer as much experience in writing carefully as an essay assignment would do. But keeping a journal helps members of the class to become involved with the reading, and may, in some cases, provide the first occasion on which they write with pleasure.

Whatever the field in which we may be teaching, whatever the level at which our students may be working, that experience in composition is one of the most valuable we can give them. Writing frequently and carefully will teach them ways of formulating, evaluating, and organizing ideas, the very skills they so often need in order to master and to apply the facts they are learning in our courses. And, indeed, long after they have forgotten some of those facts they will remember and utilize what we have taught them about writing.

CHAPTER EIGHT

Grading and Evaluation

Christopher M. Jedrey

The evaluation of students' work is one of the most difficult of a teacher's tasks, because grades have a personal as well as a practical dimension. As students, most of us felt that a grade was in some sense an evaluation of our personal worth, not just our work. Perhaps this is because evaluation in an academic setting has the appearance of precision (that is, a *B+* or a 78) and an authoritative source. We can always expect to be evaluated, but outside college seldom is this done so frequently or so explicitly. Moreover, the multiple, rapid-fire series of evaluations comes at a time in their lives when most college students are beset with uncertainty about themselves, and much concerned with their future prospects.

It is not within our power as teachers to make grading and evaluation painless, but we *can* reduce the amount of unnecessary pain caused by grading and increase its usefulness to the students by thinking a bit about how and why we grade. It is important to remember that grading is inherently subjective. Most exams require essays, not merely the recall and recitation of facts. Even in the basic natural science, mathematics and language courses, the awarding of partial credit injects a significant subjective element into the evaluation. Most college teachers are as interested in evidence of conceptual grasp as in simple mastery of the material. The results of memorization and rote learning are easy to evaluate; not so an essay wherein the desiderata are clarity of expression and originality of thought.

CHRISTOPHER M. JEDREY received his Ph.D. in History from Harvard in 1977. Since then he has been Allston Burr Senior Tutor in Lowell House and Lecturer on History and Literature at Harvard College. His thesis was published as *The World of John Cleaveland: Family and Community in Eighteenth-Century New England* (Norton, 1979). He expects to receive his J.D. in 1984 and practice law in Boston.

Leaving aside the notion of simple factual errors, grading is often no more nor less than a well-informed judgment based on past experience and an intuitive sense of one's field. The subjectivity inherent in most kinds of grading imposes a special obligation upon teachers to explain the reasons for their grades and to be willing to review them upon the request of the student. If a grade is to be intellectually useful to a student, then he or she must understand the reasons for it.

Grading is an important means of communication with our students. The university requires grades as part of the certification process for the degree, but grading also has a pedagogical function. The grade conveys a relatively unambiguous message about a student's progress, in a universally understood system of academic notation. Along with less formal kinds of evaluation of work, like consultations and comments on papers and exams, grades serve to guide and encourage a student in her or his efforts. A grade measures work either on some kind of absolute scale or as compared to others in the class and in relation to previous work. Grades are used for certification by the university, and as springboards into competitive graduate programs and jobs by the students; it would be naive to assume otherwise. But grades also assist students in the complex process of intellectual self-evaluation that takes place in college. This is the educational justification for grading, and it should encourage us as teachers to be both sympathetic and honest in our evaluation of students.

Discussion courses and sections have special problems in grading and evaluation. The most obvious is the evaluation of an individual student's contribution to discussion. At the Harvard Business School, where sections may have as many as a hundred people, instructors use a seating chart and must keep track of each student's performance in class, since class participation usually counts for twenty-five percent of the final grade. This is probably not a useful model for most college courses, though there is much to be said for it as an incentive for class participation.

The first decision to be made is whether you will in fact make any effort to evaluate individual contributions to discussion. In a lecture course with only occasional sections such evaluations may not be worth the effort. In any case, in a section with twenty to thirty or more students any attempt to evaluate individual contributions to discussion fairly will require some sort of record-keeping system. This can be done in class or immediately afterwards. The former method can seem a bit ominous to the students, and may both distract your attention and stifle discussion. The latter method requires a good memory, but on the whole seems preferable. In smaller discussion courses, tutorials or seminars, which might range in size from one to perhaps fifteen students, you might not need anything so formal as a record-keeping system. Your impressions of each student's contribution to discussion may be sufficient. Memory can be unreliable, however; particularly since one's images of a student tend to change dramatically over the course of a semester. Moreover, notes on student interests, intellectual strengths and weaknesses, help you decide how best to use their contributions to class discussion.[1] Good note-taking after discussions also means that you can weigh this crucial factor more heavily and accurately than is often done. And this is fair, particularly to students who express themselves better aloud than on paper. You can subject class participation to more formal evaluation if you assign oral reports, or give some students responsibility for extra reading each week, or a chance to conduct the discussion. Such exercises are more easily evaluated than any single contribution to the give-and-take of discussion, and they also increase the student's sense of responsibility for the course.

Aside from exercises like these, the grading of individual contributions to discussion is most difficult. What are we grading—frequency of comments, enthusiasm, the individual tour de force, or the ability to forward the discussion—and how? What weight should this factor have in determining the final grade? Although more elaborate systems of evaluation are possible, for most teachers of discussion courses contribution to discussion is evaluated·impressionistically and is used to modify grades otherwise established. Though discussion is the central task of sections, tutorials, and seminars, students are most often evaluated on the basis of their written work, exams and papers.

Exams and papers test quite different intellectual skills. Exams try to be comprehensive, whereas papers give students an opportunity to investigate some more limited topic related to the course in more depth. Many discussion courses do not have

---

1. For a fuller treatment of this important subject, see Chapter Four, "Questioning," by Thomas P. Kasulis, pp. 38–48.

exams, though lecture courses with discussion sections often do, as do certain large introductory courses which are mainly taught in sections. If you teach a section within a larger course, the exams should be a subject for negotiation, so that both the broad purposes of the course and the special preparation of your section are adequately acknowledged. You must be sure that your students get the exam they are prepared for, or are prepared for the exam they will get.

The material to be covered on an exam should always be clearly delineated for the students. To prepare properly they should know whether an exam is to be comprehensive or only since the last hourly, and whether some particular aspect of the course is to be stressed. In the making of an exam, identifications, short answers, and multiple choice questions test factual knowledge as well as a student's ability to place a bit of information in context. Questions like these enable you to cover a lot of material, and the students' ability to answer a number of these questions suggests a good general understanding of the subject. These brief, generally factual, questions imply a deeper knowledge of the subject but do not actually test it. Essay questions test students' ability to synthesize the materials of the course for themselves. A good essay question should push the students to think over the implications and ramifications of what they have learned, and not merely to recall what they have read and heard. A really good essay question—or better yet, a related series of questions—will be a learning experience in itself for the students. Writing educational exams is an art. Studying the exams others have given may help you in developing your own skill at creating exams, and can certainly convince you that mastery in this field is not an automatic attribute of a college teacher.

In the designing of an exam, the instructor should decide how directive he or she wants to be. If all students must answer the same question, it is often easier to grade comparatively. After reading several essays on the same subject you very quickly get a sense of the range of possible answers and the degrees of excellence to be found in these answers. On the other hand, wider choice gives students a better chance to show their best work. To some extent, the subject material influences one's choice in this matter. Courses that stress mastery of a body of material, like basic math, science, and language courses, are more likely to be directive than upper-level courses, which are more apt to be concerned with teaching a particular methodology and so the more willing to see it applied in different contexts.

There are also a variety of procedural details which necessarily have educational consequences. Frequent exams or quizzes help keep students abreast of their work, but they also reduce significantly the students' responsibility for their preparation. Again, beginning math and language courses often find such drilling exercises useful; more advanced, synthetic courses less so. The use of books and notes during examination in more technical courses is an important question for teachers as indeed is the use of in-class exams at all. The standard in-class exam forces the students to rely on her or his memory for formulas, names, dates, and other pertinent information. It is up to the instructor to determine how important the memorization of such information is to be.

In contrast a take-home exam puts more stress upon the use or synthesis of material than on its recall. Take-home exams are administratively messy and not usually popular with students. Student anxieties focus on the question of allotment of time (if I devote four hours to the exam, is someone devoting eight, twelve, twenty?). In giving take-home exams, then, it is important to limit both amount of time and number of pages, and, in fairness to other students, to enforce those limits strictly. The take-home exam can be troublesome to administer, and may encourage reliance on others (books, friends, lecture notes, etc.), but it can also produce more thoughtful and more readable (typed) essays.

Whatever kind of exam you choose, it should be administered with some care. You should be sure to teach your students good examsmanship, so that you can grade their best efforts. They should know at the beginning of the semester how many exams there will be and when, so that they plan accordingly. Any later changes (ideally, there should be none) should reduce the workload, not increase it, in the interest of fairness. The exam itself might carry suggested time allotments for each section, to encourage students to budget their time properly. In a more objective exam, students should be advised to pass over questions that they do not know immediately and return to them later, after answering those that they do know. The exam directions should be clearly stated at the beginning of the exam, the exam itself should have been carefully proofread, and you should plan to stay in the room during the exam period to answer questions and to ensure fair exam conditions. These may seem petty concerns, but they require careful and conscientious attention so that no one has reason to feel that his or her grade was affected by them.

Eventually the unhappy day arrives when you are confronted with a stack of hastily scribbled exams. Reading them is admittedly a chore, but it is a particularly important chore for you and the student. The exam is one of the most direct ways of measuring the effect of your course (if a few students miss your most important point it may be their problem; if most miss, it is your problem). The students, on the other hand, have just put forth, under some pressure and in expectation of judgment, the best effort they could muster for the occasion. Each has every right to expect your fullest attention.

The blue-books, or at least some of them, should be read without comment at first. You need to establish some sort of comparative perspective before you begin assigning grades. Do all you can to minimize the impact of your mood on the evaluation. You should not read too many blue-books at one time, or under adverse conditions. Do not read the exams you expect to be the worst, last; do not get disgruntled and angry when all are not as good as the best; do not save the reading for late at night or early in the morning if those are your worst times. You might try grading the exams "blind"; that is, without our reference to student names. Your personal feeling about a student based on class discussion or some out-of-class contact, or your evaluation of past work, may subtly influence your grading. The fact that Mary is attractive and lively and John surly, or that one received an *A* on the last exercise and the other a *C+* may lead you to typecast that student in your mind and to read the exam accordingly. If we want students to believe that we are judging their work, and not their personal worth, then we must enable ourselves to do so.

We should expect to have to deal at times with unattractive varieties of examsmanship. We are all familiar enough with exams, taking them or giving them, to know irrelevant, long-winded "bull" when we get it, and can grade it accordingly. If an answer seems irrelevant to the question but still coherent, it may be an attempt on the part of the student (perhaps prepared beforehand) to pull the exam over into some special area of expertise. Depending on how remote the answer is from the purpose of your question and how good an essay it is, you might want to give such an answer some credit, but in general once you have determined the range of choice available in your exam, anything outside of it is not really relevant. In fairness to other students, who may also have had a preferred topic but instead answered your questions, it should not be otherwise.

Your exam may elicit strange responses. A former professor of mine once received an exam written according to the dictates of an anti-Semitic world conspiracy theory. The irrelevance in this case of the answer to the question, and of the theory to the ordinary canons of historical proof, made the academic evaluation easy, though the personal situation remained awkward. Students may bring to your course other more conventional theoretical perspectives that you do not share—Christian, Marxist, Structuralist, for example. The criteria for your evaluation in these cases should be the explanatory power of the theory in the student's application of it to the materials of your course. According to the degree of emotional investment in the dictates of her or his theory (or of you in yours), the student may come to feel that you are hopelessly prejudiced and unreasonable. You should strive nonetheless for both the appearance and reality of open-mindedness, and criticize such a student's work with sympathy and understanding, and according to its effectiveness in explanation. The modern university is committed to intellectual pluralism and relativism. If a student cannot see the validity of any other theoretical perspective but his or her own, and cannot accept the idea of any failings in the application of it, then his or her future at the university is not going to be easy. Such a student is still owed sympathetic yet critical evaluation.

You may, though very rarely, get an exam that is blank or that makes no sense at all. If you know the student or feel that you can talk to her or him, do so, but in any event let the appropriate administrative officer with responsibility for that student know about it. According to the seriousness and the nature of the problem, various alternatives may be tried, whether administrative (late withdrawal from the course or from school) or therapeutic (counseling, medical care). In general your grade should still be based on the work submitted (or not submitted, as the case may be). However, if the student's problem is sufficiently severe yet there is still some prospect of saving the semester you may want to offer the opportunity of doing compensatory work. Such problems occur infrequently and are highly individual in character, so that general rules for conduct are hard to draw. In your desire to be helpful and understanding do not be too quick to disregard the academic failure resulting from a student's psychological difficulties. Disregarding it may not in fact be the most helpful solution; it may be important for the student to live with the consequences of failure and not have such problems whisked away by over-solicitous and well-meaning authority.

The exam will in all likelihood turn up more mundane, but substantive problems. If a student seems to have missed the point of the course, or at least of your questions, it may of course be because the student has not done the work, but it may also be because his or her best efforts are not succeeding. Freshmen in particular are apt to be puzzled by the requirements of a college exam. They have probably been rewarded in secondary school for their ability to recall and recite material, and new demands to evaluate complex bodies of information in response to questions that have no single, clear-cut answers may be difficult for them. Any student, however, may find himself at sea in a particular course, and you should be sure to offer assistance to all who appear to need it. If the problem seems too profound to be handled by office hour consultations, you might (in private) suggest tutoring. Making this suggestion requires tact. If a student seems inactive and uninterested you should still offer assistance. Moreover, your midterm grade should bring the problem to the attention of the appropriate academic officer, who may be able to help find the source of the difficulty and so avert serious academic trouble. Ultimately, of course, it is the student's responsibility to make use of whatever help is proffered; all we can do is make known our willingness to help.

The exam comment offers a good opportunity to confront academic problems directly and in detail. The comments should be as full as possible, though that can be a daunting task if the number of exams is large. You should at least point out major errors of fact and reasoning, note good points, and provide a coherent assessment at the end. The comments should praise and encourage as well as criticize, and should make clear the reasons for the grade. In most cases students will seek no further for evaluation, and your comment will be their guide for later efforts. If they do come to discuss the exam with you, your comment can serve as a reminder to you of your initial reaction to the exam and as a focus for the discussion. You should in any case make yourself available for some extra office hours after the exam.

Your comments should *never* be sarcastic or personal. It is a matter of professional courtesy to take the work of every student seriously, even when it seems clear that the student does not. You will find that most are serious about their work and worried about being evaluated, so that what seems to you like gentle teasing may be seen as a cutting and humiliating remark by the student. It is best to err on the conservative side in these matters.

Like exams, papers offer an opportunity to test students' capabilities.[2] Paper topics can be assigned, or can be left open-ended, within the broad limits of the course material. If the choice of topics is left up to the student, you should be ready to offer advice about potential subjects and sources. An assigned topic should guarantee sufficient material and an interesting and relevant question to address. With an assigned topic the efforts of different students can be easily and precisely compared. However, assigned topics deny to students the intellectual challenge of defining their own question to answer. As in the case of more or less objective or directive exams, there are corresponding advantages and disadvantages to either approach. Whether you think that more freedom or more structure will best help the students in your course depends in part upon your educational philosophy. It is important to note, however, that your choices have educational consequences.

In some kinds of discussion courses (seminars, tutorials, etc.), papers are the most important, sometimes the only, graded work. Like exams they should be evaluated carefully and in detail, and the comments should provide a clear rationale for the grade. Paper comments should deal with matters of form, syntax and diction, as well as content. When possible you should also talk to students about their more important efforts, or at least make yourself available to those students who feel the need to see you. Paper comments can have greater practical impact if you require the submission of first drafts. Since a first

---

2. The writing of papers is treated at greater length in Chapter Seven, "Teaching Essay-Writing in a Liberal Arts Curriculum," by Heather Dubrow, pp. 88–102.

draft will not be graded, students can work toward improvement feeling that they do so motivated purely by the desire to excel.

It is important in all transactions with students to be clear and consistent in our demands, to honor the implicit contract between teacher and students that underlies any course. This care begins with the small details of course organization such as syllabus, availability of books, meeting time. If you do your job properly, students will not be misled or confused, in a way that might lead them to feel that their academic performance was affected.

Your requirements should also be made clear early on. Your standards for work submitted will emerge from your grades and comments, but anything you can say beforehand about prerequisites, or other necessary background, or the level of expertise to be achieved will help the students decide whether they are correctly placed in your course. Since your standards can best be seen in application to students' work, it is helpful to students to have one or more academic exercises before the final exam or paper. Students should have a chance to test themselves, and to improve.

All of your efforts to be fair and objective, to be clear and explicit in your standards, will not make every student happy. You can do a great deal to eliminate just cause for complaints, but there will be some complaints and hard feelings nonetheless. Good grades mean approval, bad grades bring the unwanted attentions of college deans and parents, and all grades affect one's future. Some students may berate you or weep in your office. If they are acting like "grade grubbers," they have some reason to do so, and we may have indulged in a bit of this unsavory sport ourselves in the not-too-distant past.

Grades have a positive educational role in motivating students to their best efforts. Most people want rewards for their efforts. Still, some people feel that grading is unrelated, if not actually harmful, to intellectual growth, especially in small, intimate discussion courses. I have taught small seminars with only Pass/Fail grades and found no motivational problems, perhaps because the students felt personally responsible to me and the rest of the group. In larger courses Pass/Fail is sometimes just a way of limiting a student's investment of time in a course by allowing minimal effort. Pass/Fail remains an option at most schools, but the pressure of competition for jobs and graduate schools is likely to limit the spread of ungraded courses.

Whatever kind of grade you give, every student deserves a review of your decision if she or he desires. The terms of that review should be clear. You should *never* change a student's grade because of his or her need (to graduate, to get honors, get into graduate school, etc.), but only because of a mistaken evaluation or a clerical error. This is a rule easy to state in the abstract, and often difficult and painful in application to a mournful, angry, or desperate student. It may help to remember the responsibility for equity to the other students. Is it fair to "give" a grade to one needy student that others earned? And what about the students in similar straits who did not come to see you? The same logic applies to extensions or make-up exams at your discretion. It is good to be helpful, but not if in doing so you are giving one student an unfair advantage over the others. Most people who teach want to help their students grow intellectually and personally. We do that best when we grade their work as fairly and objectively as possible. In the long run it is not really helpful to teach students that they are not responsible for the quality of their work.

This is not to say that grading is absolute, but that ultimately we must stand by our judgments. The specific grades or numerical equivalents, however, are granted according to some loosely defined community standards. At most colleges, grades have drifted upward over the past two decades. Colleges, and even departments, may have somewhat different standards; as a beginning teacher you should try to get some sense of the local scale. Ultimately, years of grading and evaluation, especially if done in the same institution, will give you a pretty good sense of what to expect from students and of what constitutes excellence.

Given the pressure to achieve, or perhaps just given human nature, some students will inevitably seek refuge in illegal aids or the work of others. If you find a couple of exams that seem much too similar, you should confront the students and ask for an explanation. Such things are very difficult to prove conclusively. The best thing you can do is try to supervise your exams so that all students have an equal chance, and none an unfair advantage. For other kinds of required work—problem sets, take-home exams, other out-of-class projects—make sure that the boundaries of acceptable collaboration are as clear as possible. Students should talk to one another, and will inevitably do so. If they work together it is likely they will find similar answers. How then should they present their findings? The boundary between legitimate and illegitimate behavior is sometimes unclear, and nowhere more so than in this case. The best you can do is to explain how you expect students to complete your assignments, with or without various kinds of assistance.

Plagiarism, the submission of another's work as one's own, is usually more straightforward, because the proof lies in the textual source. A paraphrase too close to the original, with inadequate footnotes, and the quotation of original sources without reference to the secondary source where they were found, are milder forms of plagiarism which might be called misuse of sources. The more serious types of plagiarism range from "mosaic," the stringing together of bits and snatches from various sources, to the copying of whole sentences and paragraphs, to the lifting of an entire text, all without proper acknowledgment. You might want to explain proper citation to your students, and tell them about plagiarism and its penalties.

The discovery of plagiarism is haphazard. Something odd about the language of a paper may lead you to check the sources, or to recall something you once read elsewhere. The inappropriateness of a paper to your course may start an inquiry into just where the paper might have been first submitted, or whether it might have been submitted (without prior permission) to another course. Not uncommonly the plagiarism is blatantly obvious (a xerox of an old paper with a new, typed title page, a copy of something from the course readings, etc.).

If you find you have a plagiarized paper, you should report it to the appropriate authority. This is a hard course of action, and will often have severe consequences for the student. You should report it nonetheless. Plagiarism is probably the most serious of academic offenses. The whole basis of evaluation is undercut if the work being evaluated is not the student's, and the work of other students is in some sense devalued. Plagiarism subjects students who have played by the rules to unfair competition. The work resulting from the time and effort they invested is being weighed against a paper cobbled up from the work of others.

Students plagiarize for a variety of reasons. Some are marginal students, some definitely are not. In either case the decision to plagiarize reflects a fundamental lack of confidence in one's own work, and a painful fear of being judged inadequate. It is seldom an isolated act. The real and overpowering feeling of inadequacy and the moral weakness that allows the act are not short-term phenomena in a person. Informal warnings do not seem to work, and it is of the greatest importance that the student be forced to confront her or his problem now. The continuation of such behavior in the wider world may bring discovery and humiliation in a place where no second chance exists. Even if it does not, this kind of behavior continued will reinforce feelings of inadequacy, of being a fraud, in a way that may not later be subject to change.

These kinds of problems are among the most personally painful and awkward in the life of a teacher. They are also blessedly rare. They raise in an extreme way the issue of personal relationships with students. I said at the beginning that grading and evaluation have a personal as well as a practical dimension. This is true for teachers as well as students, especially given the intimacy of many discussion courses. It is difficult to grade objectively someone you feel strongly about. Your relations with students should ideally be friendly but professional. This is not an ideal world, and you may come to feel a strong attraction to or dislike for a student. You should try not to express your feelings in action. You should not see socially any one person in your class, or let anyone feel your dislike. We must strive for both the appearance and the reality of objectivity. No student should feel that your regard for them, or lack of it, has any effect on your grading.

This is not to say that we should not care for, or be interested in, our students. As a teacher you will often be put in the position of counselor, and your personal example as well as your instruction will help students to define themselves. Still, the implicit course contract obligates you to teach as well as you can and evaluate your students' efforts as fairly and objectively as you can, and to subordinate all else within the course to these goals.

CHAPTER NINE

Learning a New Art: Suggestions for Beginning Teachers

Richard Fraher

Holding forth in a public forum frightens almost everyone who has to face the experience. Veteran actors endure butterflies on opening night, and hardened lawyers find their palms moist before offering summations in big cases. But nobody has better reason to fret than the average college teacher. Actors and lawyers, after all, are trained to perform before large and sometimes hostile audiences. Professors are trained only as scholars and then thrust in front of the classroom to play the role of teacher. To say that this transition in roles can be a learning experience is to indulge in understatement.[1]

Only a few lack the flexibility to play both roles. Generally, though, the individual must adapt to the new role of teacher without very much institutional support. The assumption that knowledge of a subject implies the ability to teach in that field permeates American higher education, and one result is that our colleagues generally believe that the problems associated with teaching should disappear as the competent

RICHARD FRAHER is a medievalist whose scholarly interest is the influence of law upon the development of European society. He holds degrees from Wright State University, the University of Wisconsin-Milwaukee and Cornell University and has held research fellowships at the University of California and Cambridge University. Since 1977 he has been at Harvard as Assistant Professor of History; he is also a Fellow in Law and History at Harvard Law School.

1. Attacks of nerves are not in fact limited to beginning teachers. Even old stagers in the academic profession have been known to confess that their hearts still pound painfully before each lecture: some have nightmares that the clock hands are moving backwards while they speak, or that they look up to find an empty hall.

scholar eases past the initial nervousness. The point of this chapter is that the college teacher faces a much more broad task than merely conquering the self-consciousness of the public speaker. The first exposure in front of a class is the initiation to an entirely new set of mysteries, involving the communication, in contrast to the possession, of that knowledge.

Beginning to learn how to be a good teacher requires some mental preparation. It is probably important for most of us to concede that we were not well trained as teachers while we were being prepared as scholars. And the next major step toward learning to teach may involve the realization that the behavior which made one a good student will not necessarily make one an effective teacher. Good graduate students are like Indianapolis 500 racing cars, which speed through assigned tasks with impressive velocity and control in response to stringent, specialized demands. Good teachers are more like driver's education vehicles, which perform over a broader range in response to varying and less expert demands. It is less important in most cases for a teacher to perform impressively as a scholar than it is to facilitate the learning of students. There is both a comfort and a challenge implied here. The comfort is that one need not feel overwhelmed by a compulsion to "know everything" about one's subject and to teach it all. The challenge is to look beyond the secure boundaries of one's scholarly expertise, an area of proven competence, and to develop an entirely new set of skills as a teacher.

This task is left largely to each individual, but every teacher is surrounded by potential resources: to begin with, one's colleagues. There is a fallacy which retains perpetual appeal among younger teachers, to the effect that senior colleagues do not care as much about teaching as junior faculty do, and that students are more comfortable with younger teachers because they maintain a great dedication to teaching. It is certainly true that college students frequently relate more easily to younger teachers than to older ones, but this may result every bit as much from the lesser stature and "compatible" age of the younger teacher as from any superiority as a teacher. Undergraduates often find senior professors gracious, profound, and accessible. With a bit of courage, a young teacher can learn from these people.. Senior colleagues who are known as effective teachers, despite their lack of the common interests which help to bind younger teachers together with their students, must have made adjustments in their behavior in order to maintain an open process of teaching and learning. Indeed, virtually any professor, lecturer, or experienced teaching assistant will be happy to debate the merits of lecture versus discussion in a given course, the handling of difficult classroom situations, or the best way to deal with an administrative question. Most of the challenges of teaching, however unique they may appear to the new teacher, turn out to be common enough that a colleague has faced a similar bind. One of the best ways to develop one's teaching skills is to discuss problems before they come up and as they occur.

Learning the ropes on an institutional level can be as frustrating as trying to fashion new skills in the classroom. Colleagues and department secretaries can be remarkably helpful with details, but ultimately every teacher is responsible, especially in the students' eyes, for a myriad of course-related minutiae.

The following items make up at least a beginning check-list.

• *Availability of books.* Whether you are sectioning, tutoring or lecturing, your students will expect you to be able to inform them about the availability of the assigned readings. And you too will be handicapped if the books are not there when you are ready to discuss them. Keep tabs on what has been ordered and what has come in. You should personally check the bookstore shelves and the reserve desk at the appropriate library before the beginning of the term, just to make sure that all is in order.

• *Scheduling and classrooms.* The hour makes a lot of difference. An early morning discussion requires more caffeine and more energy from the teacher, because a large proportion of college students prefer to remain nonverbal until mid-morning. Professors enjoy considerably more freedom in scheduling than section people do, but the teacher in either case should be aware of the effect of the time upon the students. Tutors and those who direct independent study should offer their students as much flexibility as possible in working out schedules for meetings.[2] The relationship between student and teacher is

---

2. In one case some years ago the students assigned to a particularly demanding section leader discovered that the easiest way to escape to a different class was to create a schedule conflict between meetings and other activities. The teacher played into the students' ploy by offering no meeting times alternative to the hour most convenient for himself.

established on a more positive basis if the first official business is handled in a way that takes account of the students' wishes.

Getting an appropriate classroom may strike the new teacher as an unproblematic aspect of teaching, since some administrative officer generally handles assignments based upon room capacities and projected enrollments. Whether their courses are large or small, sooner or later teachers realize that the administrator was concerned primarily with fitting together the pieces of a demographic puzzle, and not with the niceties of environmental design. Check out your classroom before you have to teach in it. If the room will not be suitable, ask for a change. Small factors can be very important in considering a classroom. Is the room much larger than necessary? Students will spread out, with a majority seated toward the back of the room, and the prospects for class discussion will taper in proportion to the density of the seating pattern. Are the seats all fixed facing forward? How will the seating pattern affect discussion classes? Some buildings are famous for the cacophony of heating pipes coming to life on Monday mornings in winter. In general, it is not easy to alter classroom assignments after the beginning of the term, and the most popular hours present an almost insurmountable hurdle for the teacher unhappy with a leaky ceiling. The moral here is to investigate early and strike fast.

• *Syllabi.* The ideal course syllabus tells the student everything he or she wants to know about the course. Every syllabus tells a good deal about the teacher. The bare minimum for a syllabus includes identification of the course and of the teacher, an outline of the material to be presented in class, a list of required readings, and a schedule of the assignments required in the course. Optional materials, which some teachers omit, include the location of the teacher's office, the phone number, a schedule of office hours, a list of recommended supplementary readings, and any material relevant to course assignments: i.e. problem sets, case materials, suggestions for term papers, etc. The material contained in the syllabus forms the basis for an explicit contract between teacher and students.[3] The manner in which the syllabus is presented to the class creates an implicit

3. A more detailed discussion of the contracts between students and teachers can be found in Chapter Two, "The First Day of Class," by Jeffrey Wolcowitz, pp. 10–24.

contract and also establishes the students' first impression of the teacher. Generally, it is a worthwhile exercise to go over the syllabus at the first class meeting, if only to lend emphasis to the points which are most important to the teacher and to clarify anything which seems unclear to any of the students.

• *Office hours.* Some teachers swear by office hours as the key to success in the profession; some swear that office hours waste their time because nobody comes. The difference between "success" and "waste" here is directly related to the students' perceptions of the teacher's attitude. If the teacher's classroom demeanor is affable and approachable, students will believe that they are genuinely welcome to talk to that instructor. Students will frequently rate such a teacher as "accessible" even if the time allowed for office hours is limited by other commitments. If the teacher's behavior conveys the impression that she or he is really too busy or too preoccupied to be bothered, students will perceive that this teacher is "inaccessible" regardless of how lengthy the scheduled office hours may be. Being a good listener is a crucial part of teaching. While it is important to keep one's office hours scrupulously, it is critical to address one's full attention to each question or problem raised by a student, in or out of the office. On a purely mechanical level, it may be worthwhile to keep some light work at hand for office hours, the kind of task which can be dropped when a student appears.

• *Libraries.* Learning to use a new library system can bewilder faculty and students alike. It is often helpful to schedule your class for a library orientation.

• *Orientation programs.* Many colleges and universities offer a range of meetings aimed at easing the teacher into the process. Most of these offerings are particularly useful for the new instructor. Sometimes departments host orientation meetings which convey to their staffs the nuts and bolts of their particular programs or offer a course in teaching methods.[4]

Assuming that everyone will survive the first hectic weeks of organizing a course and getting the administrative side

---

4. At Harvard the Faculty of Arts and Sciences organizes an introductory program for new faculty members. The Harvard-Danforth Center, along with the Graduate School of Arts and Sciences, sponsors an autumn orientation for teaching fellows, lecturers, preceptors, instructors, teaching associates, graduate students who will be teaching in the future and other interested parties.

worked out, let us return to the subject of developing teaching skills. The most useful tools which one can employ in learning about teaching are professional literature, reflective self-evaluation, and of course, experience.

Reading about teaching can be the most excruciatingly boring experience, or it can be exciting and illuminating. Many professional associations regularly publish articles dealing with innovative teaching methods. The majority of the suggestions reflect a desire for increased enrollments as much as any desire for pedagogical excellence, but the occasional gem makes it worthwhile to keep up on this genre of professional literature. Professionals in the field of education crank out dozens of detailed studies, totally incomprehensible to those of us not versed in statistical analysis, developmental psychology, and the subtleties of lesson plans. But mere teachers manage to publish humane and occasionally profound pieces which can be tremendously useful to a reflective teacher. Beginning teachers will find much with which they can identify in Michael Mandelbaum's "Notes of a First Year Teacher" (*The Chronicle of Higher Education,* October 6, 1975). A classic case of a conversion from classroom scholar to classroom teacher is chronicled in Robert G. Kraft's "Bike Riding and the Art of Learning" (*Change,* vol. X, no. 6). Finally, a book brimming with wit, common sense, and professional insights into the student's learning process in the college years is William G. Perry's *Forms of Intellectual and Ethical Development in the College Years* (New York, 1970).[5]

Beyond all the external influences which play upon one's development as a teacher, the most significant factors remain the personalities involved in the teaching process: those of the teacher and of the student. Most of the teacher's learning will take place through reflection and observation of actual experiences. Some of the teacher's reflection will result in decisions being taken before she or he walks into the classroom for the first time. Consciously or unconsciously, the instructor chooses a *persona* to present to the class. The more consciously the teacher chooses the character of this persona, the more likely he or she is to create the desired response on the part of the students. A new teaching assistant, only a few years older than her or his students, might consider whether very formal appear-

---

5. See especially Chapters Three and Five.

ance and behavior on the young instructor's part creates a proper
distance between teacher and student, or whether such cues
suggest that the instructor is running scared. At the other extreme, the teacher who decides that informality is the ticket
to an easier classroom dynamic should consider whether the
casual approach sacrifices any of the teacher's options by creating an implicit agreement that the instructor will not be "too
hard" on the students. Obviously, there are no universal laws
regarding the proper *persona* for a classroom teacher; some
prefer to play the part of the detached scholar, some that of the
enthusiastic proselytizer for their disciplines, some that of the
martinet. One possible guideline, though, is that each teacher
should develop a classroom style which is comfortable for the
teacher and consciously directed toward the kind of classroom
dynamic most suitable for teaching the particular group of
students, the subject matter, and the particular mode of presentation: i.e. lecture, section, seminar, or tutorial.[6]

All the reading and reflection in the world cannot teach
the instructor as much about teaching as experience can. Students, especially, provide their teachers with ongoing lessons in
the dynamics of the learning process, and the shrewd teacher
pays as much attention to the unconscious feedback embodied
in the students' everyday behavior as to the conscious feedback
embodied in evaluations. Unconscious feedback is particularly
useful because it is nonjudgmental.

Almost every teacher who has spent much time in the classroom knows how to "read" a class. Not much thought is
required to comprehend that a lecture is not going over very
well if the lecturer looks up from the lecture notes and faces
half a dozen copies of the *New York Times* propped up in front
of the students. Similarly, a discussion leader learns to recognize
that the student who responds to a question by looking at the
lights, at the floor, or in the direction of his or her shoes is
generally not the best person on whom to call. But the meaning
of some typical forms of student behavior is not so unequivocal.
Does the reticence of the archetypal "quiet student" convey
disinterest in the subject, lack of confidence about speaking
out, cynicism about the value of the discussion process, per-

6. An expanded treatment of the *persona* can be found in Chapter Six,
"The Rhythms of the Semester," by Laura L. Nash, especially the section
entitled "Participants: Evolving Roles," pp. 76–82.

sonal distaste for the teacher and peers, or simply disinclination to speak out? The teacher may perceive a problem in such a case where the student sees none, or may see the problem in altogether different terms, as when the instructor desires class members to discuss the relative merits of alternative interpretations of some problem in statistical analysis, theoretical physics, literary interpretation, or historical causality, while the student may be waiting for "the truth" to be enunciated. There is no pat answer to the problems posed by the fact that the teacher and each of the students are following individual and sometimes conflicting agendas. The teacher can avoid some of the difficulty by helping the students to define their purposes in taking a course or in being at the university, but reaching the student on such a level may lie beyond the depth of the individual's involvement in a single course. Every teacher, nevertheless, should be careful not to send out one set of conscious, explicit signals and another set of unconscious, implicit ones. Bright students will respond to agendas which the teacher may never realize she or he had set.

In general, the students mirror the involvement of their teacher in the teaching process. If the students approach the learning process with enthusiasm, they usually do so in partnership with an instructor who conveys to them a sense of personal involvement in and commitment to the classroom dynamics. Beyond this, the reflective teacher seeks to facilitate the learning that suits each student's agenda—a challenge more complex and to my mind more rewarding than the most intricate problem in scholarly research.

Interpreting student feedback can be a very tricky business, even when the students are explicitly making evaluative remarks. One young assistant professor took pleasure from an encounter with a smiling student who informed the instructor that, "You certainly did include a lot of material in your lectures!" It was only later, in a more reflective context, that the professor understood the mixed message—the lectures profited from his enthusiastic delivery but suffered from his anxiety to cover all the material.

Formal evaluations contain all sorts of hidden traps for the unwary. The quantified "overall evaluation" given by students almost invariably reflects a higher opinion than an instructor might receive from his or her colleagues, or even from a self-evaluation. Students can be unforgiving in their attitudes toward teachers, but their formal, written evaluations tend to be generous. For example, the mean "overall evaluation" of all courses taught at Harvard in 1978–79 was 4.90 on a scale running from 1 to 7, while the mean for "instructor overall" was 5.36. The instructor who received an overall rating of 4.5 might feel self-congratulatory at having scored above the middle of the seven-point scale, when in fact her or his rating fell far below the mean for all instructors. Students expect their teachers to be excellent; to rate a professor or tutor as "good" may not be as complimentary as the teacher would like to think. Section leaders regularly score lower than full-course instructors in student evaluations, a statistic which may be a comment upon the quality of instruction in sections or upon student attitudes toward discussion sections. One final example of the dangers of statistical evaluations. A few years ago in a western civilization course at a major eastern university, the lectures were delivered during the first semester by Professors A and B. Professor A stole the show and received superior evaluations. The same evaluations gave Professor B a rating far below the mean for the college. During the second semester, the composition of the class remained substantially the same, but Professor B shared the lecturing with Professor C. Professor C took a drubbing from the students; Professor B had not spent the semester break in an intensive teaching workshop, but his second-semester evaluations soared. Clearly the students had evaluated Professor B relative to his colleagues rather than according to objective criteria. If you feel that the official evaluation form is misleading or incomplete, you can write your own. Many teachers in any case like to ask for evaluations no later than mid-semester, and they prepare their own questionnaires based on their own objectives and their sense of potential problems in the particular class.

What is useful in terms of conscious feedback, and what is misleading? There is no hard and fast answer. Superior statistics over a long period undoubtedly indicate that the teacher is doing something right. And from each batch of evaluations, you can wring lots of useful data by reading the "additional comments" or "suggestions for improvement." In general, a teacher should read each student's comments with the understanding that they reflect the individual's stage of intellectual development: a very well-read student will react more favorably to learned and allusive lectures than a student with little background in the field. One need not follow all advice. One new section leader found on his first-ever student evaluation a very faintly pencilled-in "suggestion for improving the course": "Kill T.A." The free-form comments provide the students with an opportunity to offer remarks which are not bound up with the teacher's or the administration's ideas of what should be going on, or of what should be evaluated. A perceptive teacher can glean from such comments a good deal of insight into the students' unspoken values and needs.

Thus far, we have dealt only with feedback elicited from the class as a whole. A teacher who is feeling particularly secure might also seek evaluative comments from a more specific and less judgmental group. Once the interactions within the class have been established well enough so that a visitor's presence would not be too disruptive, the teacher might invite a colleague to sit through a class and then discuss its strengths and weaknesses. In a smaller group, where an "outsider" might hamper the normal workings of the class, the teacher might announce the visitor in advance and have the visitor participate in the class as a part of the group rather than merely as an observer. The college teacher who desires an evaluation of his or her class performance without the intrusion of a visitor might seek the counsel of a member of the class whose opinion the teacher values. In any of the above cases, the teacher and the observer should ideally work on the basis of mutual support and reciprocal helpfulness, as opposed to operating in an overtly critical fashion.

There are moments, though, when it becomes almost impossible to avoid being disappointed by one's performance. Every teacher who ever faced a class has committed a gaffe or two at some point, and every good teacher turns mistakes into learning experiences. Errors of fact or interpretation are embarrassing but easy to resolve, simply by admitting the mistake, explaining the error and the correct alternative, and moving ahead. Errors of human dynamics—like belittling a student—can be infinitely more difficult. In general, an action or a statement which offends an individual in front of the class calls for apology in the same forum, since the entire class is involved in a contract which should preclude offense being given. The teacher who has aggrieved an individual student in class should also see the student outside the class and make amends, to restore insofar as possible a relationship which can help the student to learn.

Many classroom crises arise out of situations which may not be exactly the teacher's fault, but for which the teacher should be mentally prepared. Any discussion of material which might strike a sensitive nerve provides a great learning opportunity, in which students can involve themselves intellectually and emotionally. Ethics, politics, religion, race, and sexism are all subjects which can spark either a tremendously worthwhile discussion or a shattering explosion. Even at a critical moment (for example, in that dreadful silence just after a student has blundered into a comment which offends everyone in the room through evident sexism or racism), a nimble teacher can turn the crisis into an opportunity, because the instructor should know that at such a moment the students are completely immersed in the dynamics of the classroom. However the teacher handles the crisis, the students will remember it.

It seems evident that in such a situation, the sensitive, reflective teacher, who has invested time in getting to know the students, enjoys an advantage over the less skillful teacher. Good teaching does not come naturally or easily to anyone, even to those who seem to have a gift for it. The professor who attracts a following of talented students is generally the teacher who took time to reflect upon the means to reach the students on their own terms. A good teacher can offer firm discipline to her or his classes and still attract students, so long as the demand for non-complacent students is matched by the perception that the instructor lacks complacency, as well. The students of a talented instructor learn from his or her example to set aside ego investment and thus to criticize themselves with a firm and balanced judgment.

Many colleges and universities now offer institutional aids to assist teachers in self-appraisal and improvement, and a few have set up teaching and learning centers.[7] Take advantage of

---

7. The Harvard-Danforth Center for Teaching and Learning offers video-taping and consultation for teachers (all taping is free and confidential), panel discussion on pedagogical issues, a course on discussion-leading skills, an Orientation and Welcome for all new instructors, workshops to develop a wide variety of teaching skills, and special presentations geared to the needs of a particular course, department, or program. The Center has also published *Experiments in History Teaching,* edited by Stephen Botein, Warren Leon, Michael Novak, Roy Rosenzweig, and G. B. Warden.

A brochure describing all the Center's services is available upon request.

what there is, and especially of the opportunity to be video-taped while teaching, if it is available. The most useful procedure is to watch the tape with an objective counselor, during which session you can establish your goals. Videotaping can be an effective aid in developing speaking skills, in preparing special lectures, or in solving problems in discussion classes. When counselors are available, they are likely to have seen many similar problems, and they may be able to read the class better than you can: they are likely to notice your virtues as a teacher, where you may see only your faults; and they may be able to tell you what motivates your quiet student, or what to do if your lectures are brimming with information but dull. Having decided what you want to work on, ideally you should be taped and watch yourself again. Whether the aim is simply to rehearse and build confidence, or to work out some difficulty with delivery, most teachers find they achieve noticeable results this way. Even experienced teachers find the process helpful.

To obtain a teaching position means to take on an enormous challenge and a sacred trust. The tradition of our masters has handed down to us a knowledge of our subject, and the capacity of our students to learn demands our consummate effort to facilitate the transmission of learning. Every teacher owes it to her or his students to cultivate an openness on a human level, to sharpen the technical skills that facilitate communication, to enhance one's awareness of the complexities of knowledge and of the learning process, and to offer the flexible, balanced judgment of a worthy master. Every teacher exhorts students to learn; it is the master teacher who can convey to a pupil the message that one must reach beyond the knowledge of things that is merely knowledge, to the knowledge of others that is wisdom, and thence to the knowledge of self that is enlightenment.

Index